Hearts

A Novel of Memories,
Times past, Times to come

DONALD RAY SCHWARTZ

Hearts
Copyright © 2022 by Donald Ray Schwartz

All rights reserved. No part of this publication may be reproduced, distributed, or transmitted in any form or by any means, including photocopying, recording, or other electronic or mechanical methods, without the prior written permission of the author, except in the case of brief quotations embodied in critical reviews and certain other non-commercial uses permitted by copyright law.

ISBN
978-1-95737-83-12 (Paperback)
978-1-95737-83-05 (eBook)

Surgery

On the 16th of August 2013, Maishe Rosstein underwent open heart triple bypass surgery. His surgeon was well respected, well experienced. This man had trained and still taught on occasion at Johns Hopkins. Maishe trusted him and his surgical team.

He remained a bit confused. After all, though he had reached the age of 70, he had felt quite fit that summer and throughout the months and years leading up to this event. The nurses informed him he was lucky his doctors were on their toes. His condition was in the 10—12% considered atypical symptomology, only intermittent presentation. The nurses called this syndrome, "The Widowmaker."

Maishes's wife, Roselyn, his beautiful and intelligent, kind and generous flower, was with him the entire time. When he arrived that early morning he was whisked to a small room. They instructed him to remove his clothes. They instructed him to put on one of the ubiquitous and immodest hospital gowns. Roselyn placed his clothes in the clear drawstring bag the nurses provided for that purpose. A nurse placed a circular light blue cap, same as she wore—as they all wore—upon his head.

The anesthesiologist arrived. "We're ready for you," the man said.

They began to wheel his bed out the door of the small room down the hall. He and Roselyn stopped there for a moment. They kissed and said together the Shemah, the declaration of faith. "Harken Israel, Lord our God, Lord one." They recited the remainder of the prayer, from Deuteronomy 6:4-9. "And you will love the Lord your God with all your heart, with all your soul, with all your might . . . "

Their prayer took a minute. They wheeled him down the hallway.

They stopped Roselyn from following. It was 6:42 A.M.

This was his last thought until he awoke 6 hours later in the ICU, for the world had gone fully dark or so it seemed.

The surgery that Maishe Rosstein underwent that late summer's day, a delightful August day, temperate with only a few billowing clouds hanging the azure sky, the leaves still on the trees rustling soft sounds in the light zephyrs, that surgery the most invasive, to lay personages, brutal, medical procedures.

Upon arrival in the operating room, fully unconscious, the patient is laid out in the design of the Roman crucifixion, so iconic in the horrific death of Jesus and perpetrated upon hapless thousands throughout the cruelty of the empire. "When will this evil end?" the rabbis questioned, for it continued for thousands of years. The incision of the scalpel is made from between the clavicle just below the neck to a mark above the navel. The heart surgeon wants only to violate the temple of the human body, and has at this initial moment no concern for fine work, as would a plastic surgeon. He knows, in time, the scar will heal to a large extent at least. Then the musculature before the sternum is to be divided. The moment arrives to split one of the hardest bones in the body, aligned to protect the very pump muscle that gives us life with each beat, this pulse of life to be addressed.

As a carpenter splits wood, the surgeon bends to the sternum.

The instrument used to get at the well protected heart is at once aggressive, violent, elegant, and beneficent. The bone saw has a long history, beyond even Roman times. It was finely honed for its terrible amputations during the Civil War. Thence, hideously painful the procedure, as the only anesthetic ran in short supply, skilled surgeons saved countless lives. Years later, the once suffering men, healed, thanked the doctors for their lives. Two personages who advanced emergency medical care during the terrible conflict were Clara Barton and Jonathan Letterman. Barton (1821-1912) in essence established American nursing practices, especially on the battlefield. Often first to arrive following the battle, with her medical supplies, she tirelessly succored and saved the lives of countless wounded. No less a magnificent contribution accomplished by Letterman (1824-1872). Son of a doctor, he surgeon and Major in the Corps, Letterman devised much of the organization and techniques used in mobile battlefield hospitals and emergency rooms today: Coteries of ambulances, each organized with supplies in standard order; Trained attendants, standard to each ambulance; Establishing in quick order following the battle a series of first aid stations; Mobile Field Hospital for the surgical procedures; The concept of triage to address the worst cases judged as potentially viable. (For a more detailed insight into Barton and Letterman and their sublime advancement of modern medical emergency practice, see The Appendix, with resource evidence; and including resources for further investigation into open heart surgery, and the most significant contribution of Dr. Edward B. Diethrich.)

The modern and contemporary electric saw device was developed by Dr. Edward B. "Ted" Diethrich, in 1963. By the nature of its composite and invented governor, it harbors a unique feature: It cuts through the hardest of bone with a semblance of ease, but is retarded in cutting flesh, sinew, muscle.

The sternum is cut in half. Claw-like wrench-type instruments separate each side fully, the ribs attached following suit to their right or left sides. There it is! There beats the magnificent heart, provider of all life in the wonder of the body, its organs, its tissues, its cells, all its elementals. The four chambers perform their duty, to ensure that all cells in the body receive oxygen and nutrients, and all carbon dioxide and eluvia are carted away. Shakespeare, as usual, was right: "Oh what a thing of wonder is a man"; today we add, "woman."

A peritoneum sac surrounds the heart, a last vestige, now futile, of protecting this most vital muscle. The surgeon slices through it. The heart is fully exposed, fully available, fully vulnerable. The moment has come.

With its eponymous name, the heart-lung machine has until now stood as a silent sentry. Its time arrives. It is attached to Maishe's arteries and veins leading to and from his heart. For the remainder of the procedure, it will circulate his blood and air exchanges for him. For the first time in 70 years, from the moment of his birth, the magnificent muscle fails to beat, for the surgeon stops his heart. A doctor carried him out of his mother's womb in Caesarean manner and his heart, still beating from his time in the uterus, continued for his first moments in this world. Seventy years and more it had served him well; now it was technically dead, all in that room believing they could resurrect it when the time came. Only the machine kept his organs, sinews, brain alive.

The machine hummed. The doctors and nurses bent to their tasks.

Later Maishe would ponder the irony of it all. He had been given life at birth through surgery; he was being given another chance at life through surgery.

Meanwhile a second surgical team operated on his right leg, underneath his knee unto his calf. They removed a long vein. This blood tube would be used as his bypass arteries, inserted before and after the blocked coronary arteries by his heart surgeon and his team.

Not so long ago, patients suffered gross discomfort at this second surgical site. It took considerable time to heal. Over the course of the last several years, however, new surgical techniques have allowed this secondary surgery to be accomplished laparoscopic, a minimally invasive procedure.

In practically all surgical theaters and disciplines, minimally invasive surgery emerges as the gold standard of care, gradually replacing scalpel's gross open body approaches. Often it uses small cameras and robotic arms, guided by the skill of the surgeon peering into and operating the digitally designed device.

There is even a growing, albeit not fully reliable, attempt to replace or supplement the standard open heart practice, with its bone splitting invasion, with a minimally invasive design through the left intercostal rib, utilizing some, nearly all, or all of the digital and robotic tools available and newly designed. Perhaps future patients will be fortunate, for the value of all minimally invasive surgery is quicker healing, time of less discomfort, less time in hospital, and significant less chance for infection.

The doctors working toward this process, designing it in its infant stages have found that if there is but one or two clogged arteries, and they are in front as their devices enter the sacred realm, they have had beginning notable success. All too often, however, there is a third or fourth and it is discovered in the rear of the muscle, descending, that requires the surgeon to pull out, thence to proceed with the full invasive procedure.

Doctors in the clinics and medical schools hope to develop especial catheterizations, called both professionally and in the vulgar sense, roto-rooters. There has been some notable successes of these techniques, and, again, someday, they may supplement "the big Kahuna," the most invasive of all surgeries. For now, into the foreseeable future, Maishe's situation was, is typical. He needed to undergo what his primary physician called, "the Gold Standard."

Suddenly he awoke in the ICU. Awake, but not fully awake. The room spread large and paneled, as a family room or den in an upscale home. A nurse stood in the room. He observed only her uniform. Pink? White?

Something in-between with flower patterns. He knew she was monitoring his telemetry.

Then he knew his wife and son sat next to him. His son arrived sometime after the surgery began. They had perhaps the most difficult task—waiting the 5 hours 37 minutes. Now they were there.

He could not speak to them.

Tubes, IV's wires, catheters inserted in his glottis, arms, urethra, poking from his chest dove into him and spread from him, appearing as some alien monster in a science fiction movie.

He gestured. His son found an alpha board. Through the alphabet they went.

"H-E-L-P M-E," Maishe indicated. Again without warning, all went dark.

He descended into the dark abyss of anesthetic unconsciousness.

He awoke early the next morning, August 17. He knew it was morning; this room held a small window to the outside. He could not see through the window. Early morning light filtered in.

He glanced over where he had seen the nurse monitoring her screens, his condition. As if suddenly aware, she arose from her chair, her monitoring station. She floated to his bedside. Months later he realized he could not remember what she looked like. He would always remember she smiled.

"How are you feeling today? Sorry. Don't try to talk. Your breathing tube is still in. Your vitals look good. Think you can breathe on your own? Good. All right then. Let's go ahead. Now hold very still. We have to go slow, slow, careful, careful, you're doing great, just a little more—there! How's that? Breathing OK?"

"I, I think so."

Yes. Yes you are. And I'm pretty darn good too. Your voice is strong, not at all raspy. A smooth extraction. Textbook. I should write us up."

"You're pretty good. Pretty. Good."

"Uh, huh. A lady's man, eh? Well, seems like your brain's not too foggy. That's also a good sign.

"See this chair to the side?" the nurse continued. "What to get out of bed? Want to sit in the chair? Yes. Good. Let me check some things, and we'll get you there. You'll need to clasp this puffy pillow to your chest when we move. Once in the chair I'll see about pulling out your Foley catheter."

"I have a catheter?"

"Yes."

"When you pull it out, will I be able to hold my water?"

"Yes. And go to the bathroom on your own."

Maishe closed his eyes. He sighed. He noticed it hurt to breathe. "It hurts to breathe. Deep breaths. My ribs."

"Yes. That is normal. It will be that way for a while. It will always get better; but it won't fully go away for a year and a half. After a while, you won't notice it so much. Except when you sneeze."

"One must sneeze when one must sneeze."

"I like the way you say things."

Later she told him how he was stretched out, his sternum sawed through, his rib cage separated, all of it. But he was breathing. He breathed the breath of life. Life is breath. From the moment of our birth, our first inhale, to the moment of our death, our final exhale, we live our lives between these two breaths.

Except they stop your heart and lungs and your life is dependent upon a machine.

Maishe Rosstein glanced at the large chair next to his bed. It was on his right side. It resembled a large deck chair, with splayed white wooden back. What seemed like a comfortable green cushion occupied the seat. Wide cover for the armrests gracefully flowed out from the back.

He suddenly feared he could not make it.

She stood next to him with that kind smile. In the months that followed, how he wished he could recall this kind, competent wonderful person. Clara Barton's professional descendant. Black hair? Blue eyes? Megan? Miranda?

He had heard the anesthesia continued to fog the brain for days, even weeks. But he was thinking all right. He had survived. He was now in the first and second day of what would be a long recovery.

"All right, let's get you up, out, and sitting," she said.

"I don't think I can," Maishe said.

She knew better than he that he could. She knew better than he what he could not do. "Here we go. Clutch your puffy pillow to your chest.

Tight. Good. Legs out first. Don't worry about the gown. I've seen it all before. No. Out this way. Knees over. Good. Don't worry. You won't fall. I've got you. All right. Slowly now. Over here a little. And sit down. It's OK. Sit down. Excellent. I'll take some vitals. If all stays stable for a while, I'll take the catheter out. Does it bother you? No? Good. That means it'll probably come out smoothly also. All right. For now, just enjoy sitting up. You're OK sitting?"

"I am enjoying it, as you said. I, I feel a little dizzy."

"That's normal. Just sit back against the chair. You won't fall out. Don't worry. Look straight ahead most of the time. Better? Good."

Back and forth Megan or whatever her name was, his ICU angel took his vitals, ensuring her charge was progressing as expected 24 hours after the greatest beneficent assault on the human body.

He would at least remember her competence, her compassion, her charm, her consideration, her smile, her tapering fingers.

He would remember how physically strong she was.

"Should we order some breakfast? Are you hungry? No. No food yet. Very normal. Well then, everything looks good so far. Let's get this catheter out. Ready? Good. Ok then."

His angel on earth bent to her well trained task.

He had slept later than he thought. Late morning edged toward noon. He found himself in the chair. He did not remember moving to it. Then it seemed he did recall his movements, slow, as slow motion in film. He did not know how long he had sat there. Time did not process as it ordinarily processed. He knew from time to time, even sitting up, he dozed at length. The chair he realized later, was designed for one to doze, to nap, to support her or his body and head.

He was awake, or some semblance of wakefulness when his wife entered the room.

She had gone to the synagogue that morning. There was an adult bat mitzvah. She had an aleiah. She used the moment to inform the regulars that he had come through the surgery splendidly, as the surgeon had informed her in the waiting room following the procedure.

She wore a pink blouse. A red beret rakishly to the side of her head in a futile attempt to cover her luxurious crown of thick hair, now beautifully streaked with gray. They had been young together, with the joy of physical discovery over their earlier years. They had grown old together, now, hopefully would for good years left. She wore that disarming smile he loved so much. It was hopeless for him. He knew that. All he ever saw was the girl who had walked down the aisle.

"Look at you. You're sitting up. You look good. Wow. I am so happy."

"Don't feel so . . . "

"It's all right. You will. You'll see. I told everyone the surgery was a success. They all say hello. They're praying for you."

"That's good. How are you holding up? Our kids?"

"I'm good. They're good. We had a wonderful Shabbat dinner last night. We all missed you."

"Yeah." He paused for a moment.

"The house OK," Maishe asked.

"Everything's fine. You're falling asleep, I think. Go ahead. I'll be here all afternoon."

"Nurse. I think . . . "

"Yes. Let's get you back into bed. Excuse me ma'am. Thanks. Now. Slowly now. Hug your pillow tight. That's right. Knees and legs around. That's it. We'll get you to the chair again later. And tomorrow you'll walk over to the door and back."

"I don't think I can," Maishe said.

"That's what you said about the chair," Megan said. "There now. All OK? Good."

"Rose."

"I'm here, sweetheart."

"You don't need to stay. I'm just going to . . . "

"I'll be here," Rose said. She looked at Meghan.

"He's doing real well," Megan said.

"Good," Rose said. Then she sat back in the chair. She opened a Sudoku puzzle she had brought with her. It was difficult. For a time she was frustrated. But with her normal persistence, she got it. From time to time, she looked at her husband. His sleep became more regular, a good sign, she thought.

"He looks so peaceful," Rose said. "Oh. The sun from the window just crossed his cheek. So—"

"He really is doing very well," Megan said. "Better than most of my patients." She must have seen the odd look Rose gave her. "Honestly."

"Baruch HaShem," Rose said.

At dinner time, she went down to the cafeteria. She soon returned. She was by his bed when he awoke.

The next morning, Sunday, the 18th of August, he walked across the room. He walked out into the hall. His son and wife came just as he quit the room. All were most pleased at this triumph. When he returned, he was able to sit in the chair. He did not need to return to the bed, not right away.

A new nurse took care of him. She assured his family things were going along very well. He would not remember her either.

He missed Meghan. He hoped she was OK, that it was simply her day off.

Toward noon, one of the surgery team, the doctor's PA came in. This man reviewed his chart, re-examined him. What was the man's name? He knew it the week before the surgery. Barly, Barney, wasn't it?

"You're doing very well, Mr. Rosstein," Barry said. "I'm going to remove these pacemaker wires. We wait to see if we need to attach one. Hold on. Still, now. It will only take a—there. I think also tonight we'll move you from ICU to Step-down."

The wires being removed felt like thin pins being pulled from his chest. A human pin cushion. Breathing tube, catheter, wires removed. Yet he was still attached to at least two IV's as far as he could tell, something in his neck (a jugular infusion device of some sort?). He was going to Step-down. He did not want to leave ICU. It was a nice room, paneled and had a window. The nurses were competent and compassionate. His son and wife looked pleased. It meant he was progressing.

He did not want to go.

He did not protest.

Later that day they moved him to Step-down.

He did not remember the transport. To Maishe, it was a Star Trek Transporter incident. He was in ICU. He was in Step-down.

This room was small, close. Noises filled the atmosphere—beeps, bleeps, something indistinguishable, a robot device in voice mode. The nurses here welcomed him. At least, he thought he remembered they did.

That night, early Monday morning proved to be his most difficult time, almost a setback. His bed started to shake. Something large beat in his chest, as if an alien creature trying to crash through his recently split sternum. No need to worry, the nurses had told him. The two sections of the bone are held tight together with titanium wires and screws. They repeated how tight they were.

Titanium screws, gold crowns, porcelain caps, two mercury filings remaining, three wire stents from seven years previous, little cages. He was a cyborg, a $6 million dollar man.

Something was wrong.

In the morning, when a new, competent nurse came on, he described what he had gone through. She told him he had an episode of "A Fib." The night nurse had ignored her screen or simply did not care. She left him like that for five hours. His heart could have been damaged. He was fortunate. Finally she inserted a line with amiodarone, a drug to return atrial fibrillation to sinus rhythm.

At noon on Monday, the day shift nurse taking good care of him, looked at his screen and actually pranced, happy, even gleeful it seemed to him. She was a good woman.

"Mr. Rosstein, you converted."

His wife hugged him. He was back on track. He would be OK.

Later, he wrote up the night nurse who had ignored his travail for too long.

His return from Customer Relations made it clear they were covering for her. But, alas, he knew all too well the truth of the matter, and he worried for future patients in same or similar circumstances, if that person were on duty.

On the fifth night of his hospitalization, a balmy clear blue sky late summer's eve, he was discharged. It took some time for the skilled nurses to remove the last of his IV"s and jugular infusions. It all had to be done with care. But these nurses were competent, compassionate, on their toes with their cases and their charges. These women he would always remember well.

Wan was slight, clearly of Asian descent. Not only careful good at her work, but infused with a joy that permeated his small, close private room, practically bouncing about instead of merely walking. It had been she who had monitored his heart condition so closely and pronounced him returned to the rhythm that we all need to have; for this is the truism of our lives on earth: We may do with one kidney, one testicle, one ovary, no gall bladder, even part of our liver—but we all need a regularly beating heart every second, minute, hour, day, week, month, year of our lives. Assuming 70 beats per minute, a life span of 80 years, an astonishing number--over 3 billion beats. Three billion times the nerve messengers at the sinus node direct this magnificence, this jewel, this gem, this elegantly designed 4 chambers to begin flowing blood out, resting and receiving blood in. Out, in, out, in, a pulse in concert with movements of the cosmos, nature's connection to the harmonic energy of the earth in its place amongst the stars.

For Maishe, and other open heart surgical patients, there were a few less beats. An interruption occurred, as the heart-lung machine had kept him temporarily from the cosmos harmonic convergence; his and their heart(s) silent for about 6 hours of their lives. His wife brought him his clothes. He could not bend as well as before. It took him a while to dress. Rose went to get the car, to pick him up at the front circular drive of the front door of the hospital. He received his discharge instructions. Soon a pleasant young woman from Transport brought his wheelchair by. He told these competent, compassionate, happy, and pleasant nurses farewell. Soon after his room carefully cleaned, another patient would come to occupy it.

The young woman pushed him up to the exit, the front of the building. It was quick. Maishe was surprised to discover he had not been so deep in the bowels of this complex facility.

Rose drove up. Clutching his puffy pillow tight against his chest, he ensured the seat belt drew over it. He told the young woman thanks. And goodbye. Then they were off for the fifteen minute ride home.

The scents of flowers and leaves of trees hung in the late afternoon. The sky a brilliant azure with only a few small fluffy clouds. He realized his senses were for a moment more astute though he knew his full thought process had not yet returned.

He came home. It was good to sit in his chair, to listen to the soft scintillating sound of silence, the wonder of quiet. Rose busied herself in the kitchen to warm up some chicken soup. He knew he would be able to eat a little at last. He had not an appetite in the hospital. The morning's scrambled eggs looked appealing; he had only been able to eat a bite or two each of his days. It was important to drink however. He needed to remain hydrated.

Rose fussed in the kitchen. He leaned back to rest. In an instant, he recalled in vivid detail the entire story.

He thought during surgery he had been aware of the abyss of nothing, deep blackness, a deep India ink screen of impenetrable absence of any light. Now, leaning back, home, waiting for his soup in that few minutes, he knew. Then, and now, for the minute before the surgery, in this instant, he remembered every detail of the days of his youth, the days he left home, the days before he married, every minute, hour, month, year as a single young man on his own. His bachelorhood as he began to explore this adult wonder of life.

He remembered how delightful his childhood had been, how much his mother and father loved him, how certain he was he had disappointed them in his confused, dissociative teenage years. Thankful he had escaped getting into real trouble more than once.

He remembered it all, every moment. He knew he had recalled all this in deep thick blackness of nothingness while they sawed through his sternum, separated his ribs, cut through his muscles and the heart sac, stopped his heart unto the machine, surgically removed a vein from his right leg, bypassed three of his coronary arteries.

Most of all, when he was in recovery, most of all, he remembered the days of his adult youth, a single man, a bachelor, ere he married.

In the blackness, the void of the void, the deep of nothingness these vivid memories returned.

He envisioned them. He heard the sounds. He smelled the scents.

In that few moments, then, and waiting for the soup to warm, it all returned.

Most of all . . .

Days of a Young Man: Little Rock, Arkansas, August 1966

Little Rock Air Force Base is a large federal reservation. Its entrance gate leads off the main highway and cross spur of Jacksonville. This small town, occupied by many airmen and their families, and the base lie about 15 miles north of Arkansas' largest city, its state capital. Maishe had driven 3 days. He had some time between the completion of his training assignment and his assumption of his regular duty. He had gone home to spend the better part of the week with his parents. They had not seen each other since February when he had, in an emotional moment, left the only home he had known.

"Well, this is it, I guess," Maishe had said. Tears welled in 3 pairs of eyes. They hugged as they had not since he was a child. Then he was off.

It was wonderful to be home again, if only for a little while. Then came time to depart. From Louisville he passed through Elizabethtown, Nashville, Memphis, on to Little Rock. The Interstate Highway System was still under construction. One went on the new divided highway for ten miles or so; then off, returning to the old state and federal routes. So it went.

At last he came to the gate. The Airman on guard duty looked over his orders. He gave him a map of the huge facility. Then Maishe, an officer in the United Sates Air Force, was saluted. He had dressed in Class A uniform that morning. He returned the salute. There was a proper way to do it. Maishe was always sure to do it right. He came to attention, rested his two fingers over his right brow, the four fingers together, thumb along the index finger, and sharply brought his hand down close to his chest and abdomen. The Airman followed suit.

In his car, at the off-site of the gate, he looked over his orders for the thousandth time. This time, however, in concert with the base map. Though military reservations were quite large, they generally had only a few roads, so it often was not difficult to adjust to one's new quarters. Of course every roadway was perfectly paved, smooth. The grasses pristine, cut to a uniform height, the flowers along the way free of weeds.

A loud noise overhead interrupted his studious reverie. He looked up through the driver's window. He caught only a glance of them. Two F-4 Phantoms in formation, just off the flight line, probably from their climb. He perused the map. The building he would report to was in the opposite direction of the flight line. Well, he would see it at some point. He knew B-52 bombers took off and landed there on their SAC (Strategic Air Command) global missions. He wanted to see them. He would, often.

Then, knowing where he needed to go, seeing it was almost noon, and how some offices closed for lunch, he started his car. He proceeded from the gate.

It took him 10 minutes to arrive at the 308th Strategic Missile Wing, Titan II ICBM, each weapon system harboring death and destruction of 10 megatons. He pulled into the lot marked HQ, Headquarters.

The office of Major Luke Carstairs was easy enough to find. Maishe knocked twice, waited, heard the somewhat gruff voice.

"Come in."

Maishe opened the door. He entered the room. It seemed small. The man with the gold leaf clusters on his collars of the summer brown open collar uniform sat behind his desk. It surprised Maishe that the desk seemed old, wood, and etched with scratches. Carstairs surprised him as well; his uniform had wrinkles. Maishe and the young officers he knew had been taught and practiced well to keep uniforms well pressed, their shoes spit-shined. This man's shoes needed shining, Maishe noted, for Carstairs stood by his chair, raising his black socks. Maishe suspected the ritual proceeding before him repeated several times throughout the day. Carstairs was also given to a bit of overweight. The man's shirt bulged at the buttons. Maishe wondered if he had recently been passed over for promotion and seemed no longer to care for the 3 or 4 years he had to his 20.

The haircut was to code, however. The man's eyes peered small, Maishe noted when he finally looked up. At that point, Maishe once again came to attention, this time, since he entered the building, his cap caught up in his blue belt, the buckle of it perfectly aligned with the line of his shirt buttons and fly.

"Lt. Rosstein reporting for duty, Major, for Deputy Commander Combat Crew assignment."

"So you took an extra five days you weren't allowed, that right, Lt.?"

"What? No. No sir. Everyth—"

"We expected you, and, let's see, Hodges, Monalis, and Wheeler five days ago. We almost put all of you on report. You want to explain yourself?"

Maishe knew that when contradicting a superior officer, it was best to use the third person rhetorical device.

"Sir, no sir. If the Major will look over my orders, I know he will perceive the bold print below Subparagraph I-G-4: That is, 5 days allowances beyond travel times, as indicated, for, to quote directly sir, 'personal business.'"

"Give it here."

"Sir."

"Hmm. Humph. Well, they should have sent us this as well. Another SNAFU. All right, Lt. You're OK then. I'll notify the duty sergeant at the CP. Let me have, ah, five more copies.

"Sir."

"At ease, Lt. Good. You know anything about tires?"

"Tires, sir."

"Yeah, tires. See that white Buick out here?"

In fact, from when he first entered the room, Maishe had admired the open field with three graceful trees through the window, beyond Carstairs's desk and chair. He had noted that the Base Exchange area appeared to be beyond the field. Probably the Officer's Club was in that area. It was approaching one and he felt himself getting hungry for lunch. He had made a mental note how to get there from these offices. Still, he had much reporting to do: His own Site Commander for assignment to a crew; The medical facility to process the records he carried in the purple tube in the back seat of his car; Payroll of course; And he needed to acquire from Supply his special crew uniforms. He would be on duty 25—28 hours with anywhere from 2 to 4 days off in-between.

Now, before the field began, for the first time, he noted a gleaming white automobile. For a moment he thought the Major takes better care of his cars than his person. He dismissed the thought. The man was his superior officer. They were chums now in the brotherhood of cars and tires. Maishe knew little about cars and tires.

"The white one," Maishe said. "Yes sir. Looks like a beautiful car."

"Yeah, it is. Engineered well. Real well. All the bells and whistles. You know what I mean."

"Yes, sir."

"Except, Lt. . . ."

"Sir."

"It has only two play tires," Carstairs said. "What do you think of that, Lt. A car like that. I only bought it 3 days ago. I just discovered it had 2 ply tires. What do you think of that?"

Maishe knew he had to come up with an answer. He tried to equivocate.

"Perhaps, Major . . ."

"Call me Luke, Lt. Um, let's see, Mosh—Maishe, is it?"

"Maishe," Maishe said. "Yes sir. I, that is, Luke." They were chums. "Perhaps after driving a while and, well, I think the car will handle all right, you know. For a while, then you can look for a sale—I think Sears has discounts for military, and, 4 ply, that is . . . " Maishe knew he rambled. He had not remained a car and tire chum. Military formality suddenly returned.

"Here is your report form, Lt. You will report tomorrow morning 0930 to Site Commander Hayes, 74th Squadron, Building 7A. Thank you can find it, Lt?"

Maishe glanced over at where he was sure the SC would be. He hadn't eaten since the evening before. Tomorrow. Good. He would have some time left today to take care of other matters. Well, finding a place to live, for one thing.

"And here is your voucher for your rooms in the VOQ. You'll have these quarters until you locate permanent housing. Single man, are you?"

"Yes, Major."

"Well ask the duty sergeant out there for the list of Jacksonville apartments. There's some good ones across the street from the front gate. Payroll will get your housing allowance sorted out. For now, Sergeant

Johnstone will l get you a Visiting Quarters room to operate from and get some sleep at night. Linens, blankets, provided, all that."

"Yes, sir. Today, sir." Today. Obviously today. When else?

"See the duty sergeant at front for all the rest of it. Sgt. Johnson." Major Luke Carstairs glanced at his watch. "He should be back from lunch now."

"Yes, sir."

"Dismissed."

"Sir."

Maishe came to attention again, saluted sharply as always; upon its return, executed an about face and exited. At the door, he turned while closing it.

Major Luke Carstairs was standing by his chair, adjusting his black socks.

As Lt. Maishe Rosstein entered the Officers Club, he doffed his flat cap, to, perfectly peaked at just the rakish angle required, and placed the head cover within his blue belt, its own buckle perfectly aligned with the line of his uniform shirt and fly of his pant. He needed to open his account. Hi stomach gnawed. Today he would pay cash. He smelled the scents of the food. He heard the clatter of dishes and clinking of silverware before he saw the door to the mess.

"Rosstein."

Maishe turned. A few feet away stood one of his classmates from his missile combat training at Vandenberg.

"Wheeler. Hows't going Ron?"

"All right. You see Carstairs yet?"

"Yeah, just came."

"Quite an exemplary officer, eh?"

"Well . . ."

"Sergeant Johnstone was better. Knew how to get the vouchers right. Where we need to go, in good order, so on . . ."

"Yeah," Maishe said. It seemed so to me."

A Lt. Colonel and a full Colonel walked by. Maishe and Lt. Ron Wheeler moved to the side, showing proper deference. One of the first things taught in ROTC is RHIP, Rank Has Its Privileges.

"Colonel."

"Colonel."

Carry on," the silver leaf collar said. "As you were, Lts.

"You're going into the mess for lunch," Wheeler said.

"Yes," Maishe said.

"Well, let's see if we can get a table," Wheeler said.

"Right." Maishe said.

They entered the large room with its high profile restaurant atmosphere. They approached the smartly dressed woman at the entry stand.

"Two for lunch?" the woman asked. She had long black hair and deep large black eyes, eyes that seemed to indicate the mind behind them always knew the right thing to say, the right thing to do. Her voice had a lilt, a sing-song dulcet tone. It added to her beauty, which was head turning. There was no lack of heads turning in a venue with these men.

'Yes, ma'am. "

"Yes, ma'am."

"I have a corner table just waiting for you two handsome gentlemen. Right this way."

Oddly Maishe thought of the old joke predicated upon the Igor character in James Whale's classic 1930's Frankenstein movie with the sensitive, humanizing performance of the great Boris Karloff. It approached nowhere near the true rendition of the magnificent literary achievement of Mary Shelley, but the latter day jokes of Igor's "Walk this way," that is imitating his unique gait rather than simply following him in. Curious thought, with a marvelous woman in front of him, her delicious scent and female cachet mingling with that of the fine foods.

They followed her across the room to a table almost hidden behind a post. She was maybe thirty. Her long brunet hair played bouncing well with the sway of her hips. Her skirt came just above the knees. She could show those gorgeous gams anywhere.

"Here we are."

"Ah, it seems a bit—I mean, ma'am, that is—" Maishe was swallowed into her large eyes.

"Hidden." Sing-song.

"Well . . ."

"Worry not. Elroy is a most, let's see, what word, competent, yes, most competent waiter. He'll take good care of you. And you know where to find me, if you have problems."

Did she bat her eyes? The vixen! Still the Lts watched her, ogled her, walk away. They knew she knew they did so.

Except for Wheeler's steak being undercooked and the man requesting the waiter to return it to the kitchen to correct the error (and it was with some deference and dispatch), the meal was delicious. Elroy indeed proved, let's see, the word she chose at last, yes, competent. They agreed to tip him appropriately. Wheeler seemed a bit stingy to Maishe. Maishe brought him around. Maishe had had the salmon with hollandaise mixed with sundry pasta bits. It was superb, and following the fresh tossed salad with French dressing, he felt now he could take on the rest of the day. Much to do beckoned before he reported for duty in the morning.

Wheeler had been a bit difficult in the class training to be Titan II ICBM deputy commanders. Well, he could not blame the young man entirely. Lt. Ron Wheeler had majored in science and engineering. To him the Air Force's most basic instruction in electricity and electronics logic, rocketry, propellants, nuclear fission, was child's play. Why he could well have taught the course. He had to tolerate the six month training patiently. Maishe and the others came to realize he was not a patient man. They all looked young. They were. But Wheeler seemed younger, virginal perhaps, almost childish behaviors and cheeks that always seemed rosy.

Maishe played an odd internal game with himself. He felt he could tell young men who were still virgins. Something happened to a boy when a girl or a woman first honored him. His posture changed, he stood straighter, his skin seemed swarthy, his eyes appeared to hold the wondrous secret of the universe. Maishe would have laid 6 to 1 even childish, rosy-cheeked young men were still waiting and wondering.

Maishe did not smoke. He never had. Often, as in these places however, others did. Thankfully, mostly during breaks outside the classrooms. But here in the restaurant it swirled common. The after dinner smoke seemed ubiquitous. Sometimes Maishe smelled the smoke on his clothes when returning to quarters.

"Have you seen Harriston, yet?"

"No," Maishe said. Is he here?"

"I saw him briefly at the major's He came in yesterday. He's got a lot done already."

"I guess we'd better get to it," Maishe said. He had already ticked off in his mind how he would proceed—HQ, hospital for medical records, Payroll, back to VOQ, return to this Mess for dinner. Or he might try a restaurant in the town. He would not mention it to Wheeler though.

"Want to tick off the offices together?"

"Maybe some other time, Ron. I want to get to my quarters, get the key, unpack, make the bed. All that."

"Well at least I can show you where it is," Wheeler said.

"Sounds good," Maishe said.

They strolled out of the mess. They remembered to tell their hostess, thanks. Maishe was able to read her name tag this time. "Stella." Stella. He suddenly was on stage again, feeling his lead role in Streetcar on the college main stage. He felt he had nailed the character, Stanley Kowalski. There, in the hall of the Officer's Club, he came close to yelling, "Stella," as he had done for 6 nights and 2 matinees.

Now he, Maishe Rosstein, would be a principal player in the theater of the real.

There was another reason Lt. Maishe Rosstein did not want Lt. Ron Wheeler to accompany him. It was true that once Maishe understood what to do and what was expected of him, he preferred to go it alone. He had carried this thought for a while that he had a totem, the wolf. A lone wolf. Decades later, before and after his surgery he was dismayed so many wanted only to kill these magnificent creatures. But that would be in decades to come; he would join the causes opposing what he considered nefarious deeds.

The real reason he wanted to ditch Wheeler was he had experienced a terrible situation, one that could have ended his young life—or worse. This incident was a memory that Maishe carried with him every day and some dreaming nights. This memory was not in the instant of the surgery revived, but a liminal moment when one was there and is always there. Examples: his parents on a December 1941 Sunday drive, down Dixie Highway just north of Ft. Knox, suddenly hearing on their 1939 Chevrolet coupe radio the bombing of Pearl Harbor; A few years before as a college student, he meeting with a Lexington street designer for a report on planning, the man's secretary interrupting their interview to announce that President Kennedy had been shot; Decades later the Challenger disaster; 9-11.

But this one, which had occurred months before the two met by accident in the OC was personal, perhaps then more vibrant in his mind always.

They had been training in small arms. Wheeler stood next to Maishe on the firing line. Maishe was doing well, excelling. He knew he would. His eye-hand coordination had always been outstanding. He had led his local American Legion baseball league in hitting, with a .363 average. He read once an article by Ted Williams, perchance the greatest hitter ever: "Some days, you know it will be a great day, 'cause the ball comes out of the pitcher's hand the size of a grapefruit; some days you know it will be a bad day 'cause the ball comes out of the pitcher's hand the size of an aspirin pill; but it's baseball, and anything can happen on any given day."

"It's baseball," George Herman Ruth had said. "The greatest game!"

They stood side by side on the firing line. Maishe was building his sequence to attain Expert Rating. It would be one of several ribbons he would be entitled to wear above the left pocket of his Class A uniform. He brought his 6 inch Colt .38 to his side to empty the spent rounds, to reload. He looked up.

The one eyed monster gazed directly at his abdomen. He faced a loaded .38 aimed at his stomach, the man's finger on the trigger. Wheeler was oblivious, telling about the beauty of hypergolic design, that phenomenon when the fuel of the rocket meets the oxygen in the combustion chamber, spontaneously igniting with great propelling thrust, lifting the Titan II ICBM rocket with its 10 megaton warhead out of the silo.

The terror and beauty of ballistics.

Maishe slowly reached his hand out and gingerly moved Wheeler's gun down toward the ground. Still, the brilliant idiot remained oblivious.

It was too close a call. He would live to 70, he now knew, and with open heart surgery, hopefully well beyond. But it almost came to an end that day. Always Maishe would see, as Macbeth saw the dagger before him, only his, Maishe's, a bullet with his name on it. His parents would be devastated, a hero's funeral. All they would have left of the sweet boy they raised with so much love. He would never marry, never have a delightful, beautiful, intelligent, and kind child (who would grow into a magnificent man), never had three wonderful grandchildren, never live his marriage partnership out to its destiny with a most amazing woman.

Years later, sitting in a darkened theater next to his young adult son, together watching Clint Eastwood in the outstanding motion picture, The Unforgiven, the actor's/character's words as the climax would soon occur resonated with him: "It's a terrible thing, killing a man; you take away everything he was, who he is, and everything he was going to be."

All that he would know later. But at the time, at this time, to be with the man who might have killed him, or worse, was intolerable.

Outside the club, Maishe said, "It's alright, Ron. I've got my car right over here. I know where I'm going. We'll see each other around."

"Yeah, well, OK. I just . . . "

But Maishe was off, to get his preliminaries and necessities done, in order to report on time to his duty assignment on the morrow.

The Titan II ICBM Missile Combat crews assembled in the HQ building of the 308th Strategic Missile Wing at 6:45 AM. Maishe had learned to rise at 4:15, in order to prepare himself, ensure his Missileman uniform was proper; he would invariably enter the base by 0620. He drove around the flight line to arrive at the building by 0635. Air Force officers knew to be early reporting to duty. The briefing began sharply at 0650.

By 0645 72 men dressed in the special navy blue uniform of this detail that guarded the world and kept the Soviet Union or any aggressor force from attacking our country assembled in their assigned seats. Seventy-two men in the auditorium wherein the 4 crew members of each of the 18 silo complexes sat together. Seventy-two men out at the 18 silo complexes who had been on alert duty since this time yesterday and now awaited their relief. One hundred forty-four men at this wing over the two days, 144 each again at 2 other locations—Arizona and Missouri. Four hundred thirty-two men guarding the security of the free world.

The 18 silos and their underground command centers were spread throughout Arkansas and the other 2 states. One or 2 were only 10 or 15 miles from the base. Maishe's and his crew's silo complex was one of the farthest, almost to the state's northern border.

Except for bad weather days, his crew drove down to the flight line, and entered the Call 1 helicopter, the flight preferable to a long drive. Usually the doors of the aircraft stayed partially open. Maishe appreciated the changing landscape of the rich agricultural state that spread in its checkerboard fashion beneath him—the only state in the union with rice paddies and diamond mines. Always when flying over the rice paddies he thought of his fellow soldiers in the Hueys in Viet Nam going out in harm's way.

He gazed. He squinted. He hoped again to catch the flash of wing of the peregrine falcon that sometimes paralleled their flight, caught in the raptor's vision through the open portal. He hoped the glorious bird wouldn't come too close and be struck by their rotors. Soon though, invariably, sighting his prey below, in an awe-inspiring aerial maneuver, the bird brought its wings slightly into its body, and dove out of sight.

That magnificent moment occurred after their morning briefing in the auditorium, the room space, the small stage, the wooden chairs reminding him of his junior high school auditorium, a kid at that time never envisioning he would one day be defending the free world.

The seats made a distinctive random clatter as the men found their crewmates and sat down. Maishe removed his blue emblazoned construction style helmet with his rank on the center headpiece, fingered the missile patch over his left pocket, and moved to his row.

"Commander."

"Deputy. Right on time as always."

"Yes sir."

The Intelligence Officer entered onto the stage in front of the screen. The lights in the room dimmed. Seventy-two men quieted.

One day Maishe prepared to go on alert, to depart his apartment at the exact time he had calibrated. It was his habit to read the morning newspaper as he fulfilled nature's ablutions. In one of those inner pages, neatly tucked in a corner he read that the Air Force flatly denied the existence of a radical new designed airplane that could fly higher and faster than previously imagined, an SR-71 spy plane, carrying the latest technological advance in camera focal length. Unlike the U2, such a plane could not be shot down, with current ballistic advances. The almost hidden article struck Maishe with an insight he had always pondered, concerning Chekhov's Doctor's line in Three Sisters. Reading a paper, the playwright gives his character this line: "Balzac was married in Berdichev." Now Maishe knew the answer to this seemingly out of nowhere and irrelevant comment; it was what is known in journalism as a filler, something to place in column space available and blank.

Then, Maishe thought little of it. He thought little of it until his drive paralleling the flight line, his customary route to start the alert 25 hour day at the briefing. He turned onto the parallel road. There she sat—a magnificent behemoth, a Valkyrie with the ability to fly from this location to points all over the globe, a stealth machine before stealth was fully invented. A phalanx of Air Police, M-16's at the ready position surrounded the glorious entity.

Maishe recalled that the previous evening, just before he fell asleep, a strange jet-like sound overhead. He had come to recognize the model of the aircraft from its distinctive sound signature alone. But this high yet almost silent whine, barely detectable really, was different. He thought perhaps he had dreamed it—until catching sight of the aptly named ebon "Blackbird"; now he knew it had landed in darkest night.

Soon he would see its amazing photographs.

Maishe liked the Intelligence Officer. He seemed more like a librarian than a man who gave his commanding officers and his combat crews an edge in the world's chess match by interpreting the top secret images revealed to his trained eyes.

He wore horn rimmed glasses. His silver leaves displayed his rank as Lt. Colonel. Maishe especially resonated with the man's flair for drama. The images would appear behind him, the screen the cave wall with painted figures for the 73 assembled officiants. Fifty or sixty thousand years ago their distant ancestors observed the paintings and recounting by the headman of the clan, images and stories of the hunt. Their weapons had been spears and perhaps the advance of the atlatl. Millenniums passed. Now their distant descendants watched with intensity their headman--Colonel Aldo H. Harris. Colonel Harris stood in front of the screen absorbing some of the imagery upon his spectacles, upon his person. But the coup de 'tat his telescoping pointer. Pulling it from his pocket, he casually but suddenly jerked it into a long device to indicate each image on the screen.

"I call your attention, gentlemen, to these three images." The drama continued. His voice the voice of a trained stage actor, loud but not strained, every vowel and consonant enunciated. A distinct baritone, Maishe and the others knew he had them as he continued.

"Here in southeast . . . the Soviets seem to be very busy. Now this series . . ."

Clarity focused at once as did the excellent photographs before Colonel Harris commented. The Russians planned to install medium range missiles closer than they had before. So it went for 15 minutes, imagery so clear taken from such a distance at high altitude, to the point of his ability to read a license plate on the vehicles in the pictures. Astonishing, really!

". . . a BMW. The license indicates someone from the Kremlin Secretariat. Very high level. Still your Defcon Level today remains at 4. SAC is talking of raising to 3—it is day to day. Listen to your dispatches as always.

Click-click-click-click . . . The telescopic pen folded into its lesser size.

"All right, gentlemen. Your entry word to your complex today is 'fresh.' That's it for today. Dismissed."

The clatter of chairs and the movements of 73 men began to file out.

"Commander Perryman."

"Colonel Hopkins."

Maishe turned. The IO had somehow appeared at his commander's side.

"I'd like to offer your deputy an extra duty, if it's all right with you. Just a moment.

"Colonel."

"Lieutenant."

"Colonel."

"Lieutenant, I've been reading backgrounds of personnel files and you're current reports. High level."

"Thank you sir.

"How would you like to be an emergency courier for the nuclear launch codes?"

Yes, Maishe realized. He was performing again, this time in the theatre of the real.

"I understand you've been approached by the Trainer Commander down the hall, Major Moralis. You'd like that job—come out of the silo?"

"Yes, sir. It think it would be a good fit."

"So do we, Lt."

We! They had been discussing him. A committee? The Trainer and Intelligence work?

"Go ahead and get the car ready. Dep and I will be out in a minute." This was by his Missile Combat Crew Commander, Billy Ray Perryman to the two enlisted members of their crew. Billy recognized at once this conversation was for the three officers.

"Sometimes we like to have Trainer officers in extra duty for us. As you know, the Trainer is at one end of the hall, our secure unit at the other. Our main level of security is personal recognition. Think you could handle that, Lt?"

"Yes, sir."

"Good. You probably know Billy here will soon move to a Site Commander position."

"I had heard that, Colonel."

"Hmm. Grapevine, eh? Faster than any land line or radio transmission. Well, perhaps we can work these transfers at about the same time. Still you may have a new Combat Crew Commander for a little while."

"I understand, Colonel. But I'll miss, well, what I mean to say is, Bill—that is, Captain, sorry, Major, I'm used—Major Perryman has taught me a great deal and runs a good tight ship and, yes sir. Understood, sir."

"Good. When you come in tomorrow from Alert, do not go home right away. Ring our bell, come through our secure outer door, be recognized, enter the second secure door. Come and see me. We'll talk. I'll show you around. We'll walk up and talk with Majo Moralis, Trainer Director. I'll let him know later today to expect us. I think we'll be all right in a few weeks."

"Very good, sir."

"Well, Commander, Deputy. Have a good alert."

"Colonel."

"Colonel."

Again Maishe realized he had been cast in a major supporting role. He performed in the theatre of the real.

Maishe's Trainer appointment and Top Secret ESI (Extra Sensitive Information) units did overlap with his Combat Crew duties by a couple of weeks. The crew's new commander was Robert Skolman. It didn't take long for the three crew members who had been together for the better part of a year to realize things went south fast. Once Maishe observed something that sent chills up his spine. He determined that upon arrival back at HQ he would talk to Billy, his old commander and the man who had been, he later realized, his mentor.

The two enlisted men let the officers off in the parking lot. They would return the station wagon to the motor pool. Maishe put his official briefcase with its Operations Manual and orders of the day in the trunk of his car. He pretended to have some business in his trunk until Skolman drove away. Of course the man stopped, rolled down his window, and glared with that glare that Maishe now knew all too well.

"Get it checked out, Dep. I won't tolerate sluggishness or tardiness as you know. I'll put you on report at once."

"Yes, Captain."

At last the seemingly disturbed man drove off. He turned the corner. He drove out of sight. Maishe closed his trunk. He entered the building. He walked to Billy's office. Major Perryman was now their Site Commander. His office opened next to the Trainer offices. Following this interview, he would proceed to see Major Morales, to determine when he might at last come out of the silo and take up the five day a week shift job.

"Commander."

"Dep—Lieutenant. A pleasant surprise. How are things Lieu—Maishe. What is it?

"Billy, I know I'm breaking protocol here, but, well, this guy is, is—"

"Go on."

"He's abusive to his crew, to Sgt. Smithers and Airman Jonesman. Even to me for that matter."

"Here. Sit down. Good. Here's some water. You need it, just coming off Alert, I know."

"Thank you."

"Continue."

"Well, I'll return to some specifics on that. But the, I mean, my deciding to, yesterday, he went down to the lower control level of the Command Center alone."

"Alone?"

"Yes, sir." Now Maishe knew what both men were thinking. They were, at the end of day, at the beginning of shift, at the middle of everything, carrying the Herculean responsibility of a ten megaton weapon system that they had the means to launch at any time under designed procedures. The current Missile Combat Crew Commander had violated those procedures. The implications could be dire and even disastrous for the entire world.

One of the first rules learned and harped on and gone over was that always two officers or an officer and an enlisted man must always be in sight of each other in the Command Center. At the very least!

"Do you know what he . . .?"

"I quietly snuck to the stairwell landing. He was so busy he did not notice me.

"Billy, he had the Fail Safe Control Panel Door open. He was looking at some device in his hand. I mean, if some fervent religious fanatic alone could launch—all right, here it is. I do not want to be in charge of ten megatons with him. I don't think he should be down with our weapon system at all."

"Look behind you, Deputy."

Maishe turned. He had hard feeling in the pit of his stomach. He was certain Skolman stood there. He had hell to pay. But no! Sgt. Smithers, an old hand who Maishe relied on often and Airman Jonesman stood in the doorway.

"Deputy. Commander."

"Commander. Deputy."

"As you were, Sit, Airman. Seems like I have to go to HQ and see about transferring a Combat Commander to a non-combat job. Maybe an Instructor at Shepherd.

"Thank you Billy.

"Thank you, Major."

"Thanks, Major."

"When's your next Alert?"

"Three days." Maishe said. "Well two and a half now."

"No classes before then?"

"Nothing scheduled," Maishe said.

"Well, I don't think I can get anything done before that. You'll have to go on that one and be careful," Major Perryman said.

"Yes sir," Maishe said.

"Yes sir."

"Yes sir."

Now Maishe, Lieutenant. I understand this might be your last Alert. You're scheduled to begin the Trainer duty the coming Monday."

"That's right. I'm going to speak with Morales and get set up when we're done here."

"Good," Major Perryman said. "Now, gentlemen, let's go into the auditorium. No one is there at this time. I want to hear about this harsh treatment, of this Captain's profile. I want to hear every detail."

It was an unpleasant Alert. It teased out a difficult 27 hours as Maishe had fully expected. If anything, Skolman was more dictatorial. He demanded that the crew members remain at their duty posts even when not running tests or administering entry and paperwork for the workman visiting, that they had the proper classified level to enter the long tunnel that led to the awful monster of beauty resting with potential gargantuan energy beneath the great silo doors atop, designed to withstand an air burst or direct hit.

"Deputy. Stay at your radio console. I won't tolerate wandering around today."

"Commander."

So it went throughout the long tedious day. It seemed he purposefully wished to make it hard on everyone. He arranged the early sleep shift to Maishe and Sgt. Smithers. Of course he would want to sleep during the early morning hours.

What he didn't know was that Maishe was a dyed-in-the-wool night owl. Being up into the wee hours was not difficult. Sgt. Smithers, he noticed, seemed to handle it all right as well. After Smithers and he got the Control Center floor mopped and dry, Maishe went to the Deputy Commander's radio console. He told Smithers to sit back at the rear table chairs and take a light doze if he wished. Two things he had learned about Skolman. The man was a heavy eater and a deep sleeper.

It was Maishe's last Alert in the silo. He decided to see if his Russian counterpart, Yari Pavlovitsch Menov, was on duty in his own silo command center. He had come across Yari by accident once, adjusting his LF gain, ostensibly to communicate with someone in one of the other Wings. Both men soon realized they were in touch with their enemy. Both could not envision destroying the other. Both knew they would if and when the time came.

It took a few minutes, then some static, slow frequency adjustment; then, there he was!

"Maishe, my comr—my friend. Is you?"

"Yari. Early morning here. Radio wants to bounce around the skies and the world."

"Is good to hear you."

"Yes. How is fam—how is your family?" Wife? Daughters?"

"Yes. Is good. Girls grow, how you say in English?"

"Fast? They grow—

"Yes. This is . . . fast. All A-OK my friend?"

"Yes and, well—Yari?

"Yes."

"This is my last Alert. I go to a new job Monday. Help train the crews instead of being on crew. Yari?"

"Yes. I am here. I see. I one sad. We cannot talk again."

"No. Probably not."

"What is Defcon place now?"

"Now Yari, my good friend, you know I cannot—"

There was a pause. Some static, both men feared the conversation had been ended by radio interference. Then there was silence. Maishe attempted to connect with his counterpart again.

"Yari, one thing always I wanted to ask."

"Yes, I, good.

"Are you related to Anton Chekhov?" "Ah, you know this, how we name comes, this is truth. Yes. Family always tell me this. Great, how you say, great uncle or in this way. Or cousin from before. But is truth."

"Family stories?"

"Yes. Now tell me, what play you like most?"

"All four the great ones, actually. The Sea Gull, I guess."

"Yes, great play. But best in Russian, I think," Yari said.

"I am sure of that," Maishe said.

The static grew worse. Maishe could see that a message was coming in soon from SAC in Omaha, Offutt AFB.

"Yari, I have to go."

"Yes. Is, how you say, static?"

"Be well, my friend."

"Be well, Maishe, my friend."

Soon the message from the Airborne Command Post came across. Maishe adjusted the gain. The sonorous familiar voice was five by five, loud and clear.

"To all Skybirds, this is Dropkick. At 0900 hours today normal Defcon status will rise to Defcon 3. I say again. At 0900 hours all Skybirds will proceed to Defcon 3."

Maishe read the morning papers. He listened to the car radio. There did not seem to be any world tension growing that would precipitate such a change. Somebody probably thought it a good idea. Skolman would be pleased. Now he would demand they remain at post even more so. If they were not yet relieved. It would be close. The announcement had aroused Smithers.

"Well, Sgt. At least we'll be on our way back to base," Maishe said.

"Hopefully," Sgt Smithers said.

At 0645, they awakened their crewmates. The men set about final touches for crew turnover. Maishe was right. By 0900 they were halfway to the base, and their personally owned vehicles for their drive home.

When he emerged out of the silo that morning, Maishe felt as a winged creature crawling from a chrysalis. The sun shone as a crystalline glory. It was a bright new day. He was out of the lower depths. He stood again in the light of day.

Lt. Maishe Rosstein took to his Trainer duties immediately. The early courses in contemporary computer technology, electric theory and design, electronic logic with its And, Or, and Not gates served him well. The administrative offices of the facility appeared as any other office. Maishe had his own desk for the hour or two he was not in the Trainer itself, to go over crew visit orders, reports of the day's protocols, and preparations for the next day.

The complex itself appeared as a science fiction movie set as he boarded the three steps to his operations consoles. In essence, the simulation set mirrored precisely the consoles and computers of the silo control center. In the center was the Commander's Console, the large chair clearly indicating command, and the push-button indicators on his panel exactly as in the true facilities.

If the Commander turned to his left, he would see about five feet away, his Deputy Commander's Console, mostly an LF Radio device. Beyond him, stood, from the Deputy's console in a semi-circle and to his right several large cabinets with drawers, each drawer a specifically designed computer. C-1, obliquely to the right of the Deputy's console and almost located in front of the Commander, was the Launch Sequence Computer. If launch were initiated this electronic processor would take over, and proceed in a sequence sending signals to the Guidance Computer and to the Silo Doors to open, the fuel and oxygen tanks to drip into the combustion chamber for the thrust that would propel the rocket out of its cozy bed, into the sky, into space, where the re-entry vehicle, with its terrible explosive force would thence fall back to earth its predetermined ballistic path, where, ten miles or so, over a designated target in Russia or China and detonate its awful and glorious ten megatons, obliterating everything within a hundred miles and more.

It would take C-1 58 seconds to launch. Only the Commander's Console had an "Abort" push-button indicator; and if it were not pressed in 44 seconds, it would be too late, the great wraith would arise, a searing sword of Satan sent from its nest, unable to be called back nor exploded by anyone, would foment its destructive magnificence.

The C-1 process could only be started by the Missile Combat Crew Commander and the Missile Deputy Missile Combat Crew Commander turning their keys within 2 seconds of each other, along with a Fail Safe signal from the Base Operations Command Post.

The Commander's lock was in the upper right of his console; the Deputy's lock was behind another tall cabinet to the left of his console. The made the distance between the 2 men over 7 feet. It would be impossible for one man to launch alone. The Commander and the Deputy kept their own keys in a chain around their necks; each officer armed.

Furthermore, the Fail Safe signal could only be initiated if 2 officers in the Wing Command Post had turned their keys in a similar manner and situation. If the Command Post were destroyed, the signal would instantly be sent to all the missile complexes. The Fail Safe computer systems were in the lower level of the Control Center. That Skolman seemed to be manipulating something there, violating the prime rule of 2 men always in sight of each other had concerned Maishe. For the rest of his life, Maishe considered that he might have saved the world.

The Trainer, that is, a full simulator, had no lower level. There was a second room behind the crew's console area that had a few devices resembling that lower level.

With its own push button array, analog tape run, and buffer control switches, located in a small room with windows allowing view to the "Command Center," the Trainer, the trainers, Instructors, and Standardization evaluation crews could run 3 hour exercises, creating hazards and problems for the crews to solve and resolve and be properly certified for their Alerts, which, in no uncertain terms, defended the nation.

Following his own 10 day training on the fascinating device, it emerged Maishe's domain.

As a duck to water, Lt. Rosstein thought. Once more he directed his actors, actors in one of the most important theaters of potential war, theater of the real.

Following his last alert, his return to base, to the building above the flight line that held the auditorium for crew briefings, the Top Secret Crypto-Document Control Center that Maishe would also soon be a part of, the Site Commander's offices, the Trainer personnel offices, the sophisticated simulator itself, a classroom for instruction and testing, which doubled as a meeting room, a coffee lounge (Maishe would be responsible on his 0515 to 1300 shift to start the coffee pots upon opening the building), and, of course, several bathrooms. He proceeded to the Trainer offices for his meeting with Major Moralis, the Trainer Director.

"Well, Lt. your last Alert, eh?" The man was large, with a reddish complexion, with a bit of a moon face. Odd, Maishe thought, with the Air Force dentist available, his front teeth had a gap. He told awful jokes and snickered at them himself.

"Yes sir, "Maishe said.

"Ready to come be a Trainer Operator, eh?"

This last term seemed to indicate the man came from the eastern mountains, probably West Virginia, maybe eastern Kentucky. Maishe, from Kentucky, and with his training in phonetics, could usually detect regionalisms.

"Yes sir. Right away, Major."

This was true, but both men knew the truth of the matter. It was a Tuesday afternoon. Though he would not go on Alert again, he was this one last time subject to the AF Regulation: Following Alerts, every crew member was required to get a minimum of 36 hours rest. The earliest Maishe could report for his new duty would be Thursday.

"Thursday morning, Major."

"Let's say 1100 to noon. Our best man, Captain Franks will be on duty then. He'll train you right. A good man training a good man in the Trainer, eh?" The inevitable snicker though the gap teeth.

Maishe forced a bit of a smile and a snicker. Best to start out on the right foot with the new boss.

Maishe was already aware of his schedule when he would be certified on his own: A Shift, open the Trainer and fire it up at 0555 (again, opening the building and getting the coffee pots started 0515 to 0530)—this for the 5 business days of the week; B Shift, report to office at 1100, Trainer duties 1200 to 1800, complete paper work in office until 1830 to 1900; C Shift, report in office at 1700, Trainer duties 1800 to 1159 hours, process paperwork, and close the unit, the offices, and the building by 0300 (unless TS Crypto had an emergency watch. Saturday and Sunday the Trainer was closed, albeit for his TS Crypto duties he would most often be on 24 hour call.

Maishe knew that he and other military personnel had uncommon circadian rhythms. None of the men he knew would do well with an 8:00 or 9:00 to 5:00 "normal" hours. He was already looking forward to it, to the week to week shift.

"That will do very well, Major."

"Good. Well, you've been here on the receiving end as a Combat Crew member. Now you'll see the other side of the glass. Thursday, then, say 1115 hours or so."

"Major." Maishe knew his military training demanded he report at 1100 hours. Always be early and you'll never be late, he recalled Colonel Evans, one of his ROTC instructors, always saying.

"Have a good alert rest, Lt. Your last. Enjoy it."

"Yes sir. I will."

Maishe started to salute. He was told they work as a team here; that formality was not necessary. He turned to go.

"Oh, Lt."

"Sir." Maishe stopped at the door. He turned.

"You've had the silver bars almost 8 months now, eh?"

"Yes sir. About that."

"Well, we like to have captains at rank here, working with Instructor crews and Standboard and all. After Franks signs you out and you're on your own with them, I'll put you in the first cycle. No issues, in your personnel file, I presume?"

Maishe had a flashback to elementary school. One of his teachers, maybe Miss Friend in 4th Grade explained that they all had a Permanent Record. Odd the things we think about and suddenly recall sometimes.

"No sir. No issues."

"Good. Well, Thursday, then, Lt., eh?"

"Thursday, Major."

Maishe turned. He quit the room. He walked down the hallway past the other offices and rooms until he reached the Top Secret CSI door. He turned left down the short hallway, past the coffee lounge, where some airmen were relaxing, out the door to the parking lot. For the last time as a crew member, he drove out of the lot, down the flight line, to the road that would take him out the base gate and to his apartment. A B-52 was slowly coming in for a landing. Maishe watched the beautiful winged giant, awed at the skill of the pilot controlling the behemoth. Then he turned right. He drove away.

Usually, when Maishe came off Alert and drove to the base gate to continue on to his apartment, it was over the noon hour. He had been up all night, felt his hunger pangs, and wanted food and sleep, in that order. Today he was later than usual, but he could still meet the pattern he had established.

Across the highway from the base entrance, along the road that led into the town of Jacksonville, there stood a hamburger stand. "Minuteman Hamburgers" the board over this shack read. On the sign was that ubiquitous and expected blue colonial-revolutionary minuteman with his tri-corner hat and musket at the ready. It was of course a commercialization, yet Maishe always felt a connection to the soldier. There was, after all, a direct link from those valorous men (and some women) of the Continental

Army, that army that had defeated the most powerful country in the world, largely for an ideal.

Well, for commerce and trade and prosperity as well, of course. Still, there was something of a lineage connection. Maishe felt it.

Maishe drove onto the gravel lot to get his lunch, his late lunch this day, order to go. It was the only way the place sold its products. He exited his vehicle. He had to cover, so he still wore his SAC emblazoned construction style helmet with his rank just above the bill. A bit late this day, he noted the queue at the window slot was not quite as long. In the queue stood other airman of various rank, teens apparently running down for a quick bite from the local high school, a couple of businessmen still conducting their affairs as they waited and advanced in the line. He could not help noticing a young woman in a mini skirt four in line ahead of him. He watched her enter her car when the worker called for his turn. A pretty redhead, gorgeous, I wonder if she—"What?"

"Your order please."

It was another pleasant woman's voice but heavy with clear expression. He could never fully make her out behind the dark screen, which reminded him of a stage scrim.

"Yes, ah, well, two please. And a medium order of the curly-q fries.

The voice waxed a bit louder, more efficient, but still quite feminine.

"Two and one."

The bag with his order passed through the next slot in only a minute. Maishe considered the double entendre, the expeditious and eponymous nature of the gratifying transaction. He handed the female hand the two dollars. He quit the windows. He returned to his car on the gravel lot. The two businessmen approached the window. With the enticing and seductive odors wafting about and the goods in his sack, Maishe was hungrier even than before.

He drove his car the eight blocks to his apartment, a small but classy place his per diem of $350 a month almost covered fully. A front room, spacious, and a rear room the same with good closet space. Between these rooms a small modernist kitchen and well appointed bathroom.

Maishe had not bought much furniture. He kept his place minimally appointed. Rather than a full bed, he bought a single twin sized mattress he simply lay on the floor. It doubled as a katami style seat for his one low (coffee) table and his bed at night, or napping. The telephone was at the head of the bed, for those days he needed to be within four rings. That requirement would come later as he entered Intelligence.

A few other appointments included his 26 inch black and white TV and back in the courtyard, the kidney-shaped complex swimming pool.

He set down his briefcase in the rear of the closet. He would no longer need it. He removed his helmet and boots. He loosened the buttons of his shirt. He returned to the living room, the front room. He picked up his food. Good. Still hot. He turned on the TV. He turned the dial until he found an old movie on one of the four channels. He adjusted the rabbit ears antenna to acquire from the air decent reception. He sat. He opened the bag. He ate.

The Minuteman hamburgers were always well done, crisp and layered with the restaurant's especial barbecue sauce. They were marvelous delicacies. Decades later, even food-averse following his surgery, he could still taste them and the crispy curly-q fries with a unique seasoning.

So delicious!

So here he was, not yet 25, a bachelor with one of the world's most important jobs and good pay besides in his own apartment. Of course he missed home and his parents. But he was on his own now, and sometimes felt good about it. Occasionally his old dissociative affliction reared its ugly head. But it always passed sooner or later.

Sundays became the worst day of the week. During the week, even Saturdays, he enjoyed his solitude, his work, his interactions. But on Sundays, it transmogrified to a chilling and oppressive loneliness, a gray fog as thick as Peer Gynt's great bog. He looked forward to Monday.

For now, he continued to finish the delicious cuisine. He drank a diet coke, called Tab in those days. He checked his calendar. Yes, after tomorrow, he reported for his new job, one he found himself anticipating. Actors with a script and he directing a show, this time designed literally to keep the nation and the world safe. He felt the Continental Army Minutemen were smiling at him.

He removed his shirt. He changed to his civilian sweat pants. He lay down.

He slept for five hours.

Captain Lorenzo Franks proved an excellent instructor. Maishe watched. He listened. In the evening, he studied the ops manual. In a week, he was ready to assume his own shift. Franks moved to C Shift the next week. Maishe would start on his own in B Shift, in the middle of the day.

Maishe knew most of the men on the Instructor Crews, and the Combat Crews, coming in for training and certification. The instructors brought in the problems and scenarios they thought Standboard would be addressing the crews for their certification. Maishe took those scenarios, and translated the indications to setting the new digital push-button panel in concert with the analog tape run and buffer system. From his booth, slightly above the crew floor, Maishe and his client Instructor or Standboard crews could observe if the desired lights had illuminated or extinguished. They heard the subject crew's conversations as they investigated the appropriated troubleshooting charts, and proceed to resolve the problem or problems to keep the complex in Ready status.

So it went throughout the day. One crew in for nearly three hours; this at 1201 to 1445, the next 1501 to 1745. By 1755, Maishe had returned the systems to their opening and standby modes for the evening shift. Soon his replacement entered the Systems Control Booth.

"You're Maishe Rosstein, the new guy?"

"Yes," Maishe said. He read the burly man's name tag. He had heard the name. "It's Ro--Rom—"

"Roger," Roger said.

"Roger," Maishe said. "Now I remember."

"How did your flying solo day go?"

"OK, for the most part. On the Guidance Lock problem, one of the buffers bounced back. I held it up while the sequence ran. Buffer switch 13. I'll write it up. I don't think either subject crew or Instructor crew noticed."

"Good work," Roger said. Be sure to put that in the report, as you say. Sergeant Hancock will fix it. He can fix any of this stuff. You've met Hancock, right?"

"Yes," Maishe said. "Seems competent all right. A bit talkative I suppose."

"That's him. Ok, any other problems?"

"No. Well, that A button on the push button panel sticks a little. I find if I bounce it a bit, it responds all right.

"You figured it out. All right then. I need to prepare for the next onslaught."

"Right. Tomorrow, then," Maishe said.

He quit the Trainer. He proceeded to his desk in the adjoining office. It would take him about 45 minutes to complete his report and leave it on the Major's and Sergeant Hancock's desks. He knew the 2 men kept 1000 to 1700 hours, excepting emergency.

When he finished he glanced at his watch: 1900 hours. He leaned back. He stretched. Tomorrow he would come in to work again at 1100 hours.

He thought tonight he would stop at the Colonel Sanders Kentucky Fried Chicken place just down the road from his apartment. He already knew his order—4 pieces white meat, mashed potatoes, cole slaw.

He had picked out a new book he had heard about. While he ate he would watch a little TV. He would write a bit, continuing his stories. Then around 2400 hours he would read for an hour or so before going to bed for the night.

What was the name of the book again? Oh. Right. The Andromeda Strain, by a Michael Crichton. Something about bacterial invasion.

It was time to go home.

So the days passed as days go by when one works meaningful work. In addition, though he was no longer on Alert in the missile silo complex, he felt he was still helping to defend the nation.

As with any job, the longer one does it, the better s/he gets at it. Soon, Franks was transferred, and he was the Operator the Instructor and Standboard crews came to, to assist them in developing and designing their proscriptions. He had become not only competent, he began to employ his vibrant imagination to develop the systems in ways not yet perceived. His writing needs were employed, as he added to and edited for clearer detail the Trainer Operations Manual.

Requests came by phone or telex from the two other Titan II bases Trainer personnel.

He found he liked the shift changes week by week. For A Shift, as he drove through the gate down toward the flight line and around to open his building, start the coffee, open the office and click the Circuit Breakers for the 12 minute warm-up the Trainer electronics took. He might pause for a moment by the side of the road, in awe at Homer's rosy-fingered dawn over the eastern sky. For B and C Shifts, it was good to sleep in and have a light breakfast.

One day, only a few weeks after he started, his immediate supervisor called him to his desk. It was 1100 hours. He had just arrived for his B Shift duties.

"Been hearing some good things about you Lt., eh."

"Thank you Major. I do think it is working out well."

"Seen the Promotions List yet?"

"No sir. I don't . . . I mean I . . . "

"Here. Take a look."

Maishe accepted the thick computer printout. He began to flip though.

"Page 163, Lt. I mean, Captain."

And there it was. To Captain rank. First Lieutenant Maishe S. Rosstein.

"Why! I mean . . . thank you, Major."

"Yes. You'll need two bars now, not one." His Trainer Commander pulled something out of his desk. He opened his large reddish hand. "Here, Captain. You can borrow my old ones until you get our own. Step closer. I'll remove those and pin these on."

They completed the transformation ritual in short order.

"Thanks again, sir."

"You bet, eh. Now before your Trainer shift, Colonel Hopkins wants to see you. Seems you're going to be a Documents Carrier and Intelligence Liaison, eh."

Maishe walked down the hallway to the mysterious TSCESI Control. Colonel Hopkins was the Intelligence Officer who gave the crews their morning briefing. Now he, Maishe Rosstein, from the Highlands in Louisville, Kentucky, would be privy to the country's closest guarded secrets.

He stood in front of the steel door. He pressed the buzzer. Five seconds passed. A voice came through the speaker to the side.

"Identification."

"Lt.—Captain Maishe Rosstein, for Colonel Hopkins." Then he added, "By request."

There was a buzz. A sound as a lock unlatching clicked. He turned the knob. The heavy door swung open. He entered an alcove between the steel door he had just entered and another not two feet in front of him. To his left, a small window door slid open. A serious looking moon-faced

Major peered at him. ECU, Extreme Close Up, Maishe thought, for he was always considering in his mind photographic imagery and motion picture camera directions.

"Present your AF ID Card."

Maishe extracted it from his wallet. He held it up to the window. The slit of the window closed. The second door unlatched.

He walked through.

It was a busy place. Officers peered through loups at photographs, others at documents, others typing at the Telex machine.

Colonel Hopkins came up to him.

"Captain. Welcome aboard. Come on, I'll show you around. We'll talk."

It was all a good feeling, to be part of the inner circle, to be part of the group accepted, something he had never fully known.

It was a good bachelor life, he supposed. Yet on weekends, the old dissociative affliction asserted itself.

Later, in week's end, deep into the evening, he knew. He missed his parents; he remained homesick.

Sally

Early in his Missile career, Maishe determined to investigate the largest city in the state, the state capitol. He was surprised to learn that the governor was a Rockefeller. The capitol grounds had a beautiful arboretum and a duck pond. People walked by. They brought items to feed the ducks. The ducks emerged from the water. They waddled to those tossing the handouts.

One of his major discoveries however, was an old stalwart and staid hotel in the heart of downtown, the Raimond. There he could spend fully a fulfilling afternoon.

Maishe enjoyed dining with family and friends. Maishe enjoyed dining alone with the newspaper of the day. The café or coffee shop reminded him of the Brown Hotel Coffee Shop on the corner of Fourth Street and Broadway in Louisville. Fourth Street was the action center of the city, especially Derby Week. Indeed, during Derby Week only a couple of years before entering service, he had met President Lyndon Johnson at the Sealbach Hotel at Fourth and Walnut. Wait, the old man recovering thought, I think Walnut is now Muhammed Ali Boulevard. Then he was back a young man in Little Rock at the hotel restaurant.

After a few visits to the coffee shop it was clear he was considered a regular. The smiling waitress with her locket charm, an attractive blond woman with a figure in Kentucky they called pleasingly plump, brought him his menu to the rear table by the window. Waiting for his order he could gaze out the window at the folks walking by, and read his paper.

His favorite dishes were salad with French dressing, Salisbury Steak, well done, vegetarian green beans (made to order even in those days) and garlic whipped potatoes with a touch of mushroom gravy. Sometimes he would order the meatloaf well done, with the tomato sauce. The food delicious; the service competent, with some dispatch. The price reasonable.

He was never quite certain if he should ask Sally, the attractive, obviously kind waitress out. She was a few years older, but that wouldn't matter. He always decided against it; he wanted to continue enjoying good service and delicious food; who knows what would happen if they dated, then later broke up?

He contented himself with the banter and repartee they engaged in, the compliments he gave her, ensuring that the majority of these fell upon the quality of her work. He could tell she liked that. He would watch her leave his table, her pony tail bobbing back and forth, the polyester material of her waitress uniform swishing about. He imagined his hand at the bottom of her skirt, rising up over those full smooth thighs unto that most amazing organ in all the human body . . .

He could not let his food grow cold. He ate. He drank (he had to especially request the iced tea not be sweetened, an unusual request in the south then and even now, in some places). He left her a good tip. He paid the cashier, a young woman with short black hair who always seemed to be scratching her legs.

Sometimes, before he ventured home, on occasion he was not on call, he walked across the hall to the hotel barber shop, then across the street to the movie theater.

The barber lived and worked only fifteen miles from the base; he knew how to give a military haircut.

It was at the old grand and still grandiose movie theater he first saw Planet of the Apes, with Charlton Heston, and Ice Station Zebra, with Rock Hudson and Ernest Borgnine.

He enjoyed watching the films in that theater of the olden days. The screen was large, the sound clear, and it seemed always few other patrons.

Then home again to the sanctuary of his apartment.

Becca

At least two weekends a month he had to stay at home; or, if he went out, it had to be somewhere he could get to a telephone within four rings. This was part of his duty in the TSCESI (Top Secret Crypto Extra Sensitive Information) Offices. By Saturday night he felt the gray fog of dissociation falling upon him. He knew it and the almost overwhelming oppressiveness of loneliness loomed. Already he looked forward to Monday when the fog would begin to dissipate and he could again feel solitude and joy within himself when alone.

On the weekends he did not have to remain tethered to the telephone, he determined to drive down to Little Rock toward midnight. He had discovered a 24 hour restaurant there, just off the freeway, a chain he was familiar with—Toddle House.

On one of these excursions as was his habit, he drove past it to see inside. It appeared as a vision, much like that Edward Hopper painting, with a few patrons on stools at the counter, and one worker engaged behind.

He drove around to return across a wide median. There was a large city park to his right, where he parked on the street. He gazed across the median, a broad greensward at the edge of the city. The streetlamps dimly washed barely perceptible spots, as if a mad, selfish lighting designer refused to give her actors enough light to be rightly seen. Still, he thought of the great entertainer, Jimmy Durante, how the brilliant comic-musician would, with perfect timing, stroll in and out of the spots illuminated in a certain pattern on his stage.

The bright lights within the restaurant and its gaudy neon sign without cast the beacon across the double roadway, as a lighthouse ensuring the safety of ships and those of the sea.

He liked crossing the median. He walked gingerly under the canopy of trees, oaks and maples he thought. He crossed the last street. He entered the establishment through the glass doors. They pushed open easily.

Enticing odors of fried and grilled foods struck him at once. The counter curved in a semi-circle to one end where it ended in a bit of S-shape. The stools with red comfortable cushions atop silver stands welcomed one who wanted sufficient space for privacy, but fell close enough so conversation could ensue with one's fellows. The counter top seemed pale blue with geometric shapes in various colors. When he ran his fingers over it, it felt clean, smooth. The workers, a person discharging duties as order taker, cook, and server, seemed to do the job well. Usually it was a man in white apron and white cap. This night he would remember he noticed the young woman right away.

He sat at the right end of the counter, at the end of the curve. In this way, though she assiduously concentrated on her work, her griddle cooking and French Fry preparation, he could make her out plain.

He didn't know exactly what was so alluring about her. She was not pretty, not exactly. Her mouth and jaw housed slightly buck teeth, so that he was reminded of a horse or a pony. Her hair had fallen a bit in the back. No doubt earlier in the evening she had pinned it up with a clasp. Her arms were thin, but he could see the muscles rip, wiry from the job no doubt. She wore the ubiquitous light blue seersucker servicer's uniform. The skirt, just above her knobby knees. Like her arms, her thighs and calves were thin and muscle toned. Her breasts pushed her blouse out only slightly. That was all right. A young man, Maishe already was aware that most women simply did not understand that to most men size really doesn't matter.

She scooped the sizzling burgers expertly onto the waiting open buns. She placed the order's specialty items upon the meat, still sizzling. She closed the bun to form the sandwich. She lifted the plate. She presented the dish to an older woman at the far end. This woman wore a nurse's uniform. Probably she had just left her long, tiring shift at the hospital, a bite on her way home.

Three additional customers sat at the counter: A couple not saying much to each other, perhaps trying to reconcile an argument (didn't seem to be going well, if that was the case); A young man about his own age a couple of stools removed. The young man looked at Maishe, almost peered at him. Maishe looked away. He tried not to look back at the young man, knowing he would lock eyes with him. Often he succeeded. At times he did not. Quickly he looked away.

He liked the bony-graceful way the girl moved to her customers. He liked the way she wound her way behind the curving counter toward him.

"Coffee?"

"What? Oh, um, hmm, not right now," Maishe said.

"What can I get for you?"

Yes, slightly buck teeth. Bony. Wiry. No doubt odiferous of burgers, fries, and onions. What was alluring, seductive?

"Hamburger, a little onion, tomato, pickle," Maishe said.

"Fries?"

"Yes, please."

"Large or small?"

Then he knew, at least part of it. It lay deep in her eyes, large brown saucers on a nearly horse's or pony's face.

"Large or small fries?"

"What? Oh, sorry. Lar—uh, small."

"Be a few minutes."

"Right," Maishe said.

Again, he enjoyed watching her move in that boney-graceful swish and swoosh to the cook griddle. She opened the freezer. She retrieved his order. She placed it on the grill. She threw in the fry basket his order of fries. Expert. Efficient. Alluring.

The scents and the sizzle and the sights stimulated his saliva, his appetite. We are all merely Pavlov's dog, Maishe thought. This young woman was perhaps a better physiologist than the Russian scientist.

She flipped the burger. She shook the basket of fries. Soon enough she scooped his burger upon its bun. She placed his order of specialty items upon it, the onions, tomato, pickles. Soon she would bring him food, as women had done for men from time immemorial.

"Do you come here much? I come here often. I haven't seen you in here before. You know."

It was the young man two stools down the row. Maishe turned to him. He wanted to watch the girl. Now he had to turn to this man. Now he must converse with this odd fellow. Well, he was probably also a nice guy.

"Sometimes. Saturday night life mostly. If I can," Maishe said.

"I see," the young man said.

Maishe noted he was slight, and, in contrast to the Toddle House girl, his eyes were small, beady almost. Still, it was slightly unnerving the way he kept looking at Maishe. He turned his head. She was getting close to completing his order. Soon she would bring it over. Oddly, he realized for the first time he was hungry.

"It's a good thing to come to a place you can meet people, talk to the and, well, enjoy each other's company. You know."

"I suppose so," Maishe said.

"Here's your order, hon," the not so seemingly pretty, fully alluring woman said as she placed his order in front of him. He liked the little click on the counter the plate sounded. He reached for the pepper, mustard, ketchup. They appeared to Maishe as soldiers at attention on inspection, in a wire cache to the side of the metal box from which he pulled the napkins. He opened the bun. She prepared it, served it right. He extracted some pepper. Maishe put pepper on practically everything. He shook the mustard so the spice would not run watery and would instead emerge full, hearty. He squeezed some mustard on the burger, already covered in the onion, tomato, pickle. He squeezed ketchup on the meal. He grabbed the sandwich. He took a bite. He swallowed. He spread ketchup on the French fries. He ate a few potatoes.

"Ma'am?" Maishe called to her as she walked by again. She had just served the couple their pie slices. Either their desert or that is why they came in for coffee and pie.

"Yes?"

"Could I have some, that is . . . (those eyes! Those arms! Those legs!) . . . a cup of coffee." He wanted to be awake for the fifteen mile drive back on the freeway.

"Here you go." He arm bent as she poured the coffee into the white cup with a bit of a flange at the top. He knew this coffee was good, very good. Of an instant, her fingers touched his as he reached for the cup handle. He watched her bony grace swish walk back to the griddle.

"How is it? The young man asked.

"What? Oh." Maishe had almost forgotten him. He realized this man had been looking at him the whole time. Only later did he recall it seemed to be in the manner most men peer at women. "It's good. Delicious actually."

"That's good. Yes, you see, good food, good company. It's important. You know."

"I suppose so," Maishe said.

Maybe, well, my name is Stephan."

Maishe continued to eat his delicious food. "I am, my name is Maishe."

"M, Mash—"

"Maishe. The a, as in 'bake'."

"Maishe."

"Yes. Stephen." Well, perhaps he was just a friendly guy. The fries were wonderful. Crispy outside, soft, hot inside. Maishe looked at Stephan. Small pig eyes, small hands. Slight, I guess you'd say. He did not perceive the pock marks on his face at first.

So Captain Maishe Rosstein ate his food at the all night diner. For a moment, he felt Hopper was just outside the windows, painting him and his fellow late night hawks.

The two men talked some more about friendships and so on. Soon Maishe was done. He waved to the young woman. She brought the check. $1.75. He gave her $2.00. He left the quarter she placed on the counter. He added one dollar for her. That wonderful thin bony body; he had an image of her—

"Done? Well, new friend, eh? You know. Come on over. It's not far. I have some great soft records, dim lights.

"Well, for a little while," Maishe said.

They quit the joint through the glass doors. The cook-waitress-server was busy with a customer who had just entered, an old man in a red cap. The nurse was on her third cup of coffee. The couple sat, needing to talk and unable to.

They crossed the median toward the park.

"It's not far," Stephan said. "There are some alcoves over there, in the park. No one will bother. . . "

Then, as if a thunderbolt hit him out of the dark night sky, Maishe knew the whole story at once! He began to shake. He fairly quivered. He almost cried.

"Stephen." His voice different, now, deeper, words measured.

"Yes, Maishe." His voice different, an octave higher.

"I'm only going to say this once. I just got the whole picture. Now, I do not want to wind up in jail tonight, and I suspect you do not want to wind up in the hospital. I think you'd better—"

Maishe Rosstein did not need to say more. Stephan ran, faster than he had seen anyone run into the park, a slight figure disappearing into the dark, absorbed.

The speed of his disappearance brought to mind that magnificent passage from Conan Doyle's *The Hound of the Baskervilles*, the indomitable Dr. Watson's description: "I have been to the wars, and I have seen men run. I have seen them run in shameful cowardice; I have seen them run with distinguished valor. But never saw I a man run as I saw Holmes run that night as he chased across the moors that abominable hound."

Well, Stephan was no Conan Doyle, nor Watson, nor Holmes. But he, Maishe, truly had never seen a man run like that, then to know how to absorb into the darkness of the park. Clearly it was not the man's first escape. Ironic, for the park was the Douglas McArthur Park, named after the general of World War II and Korea. The old soldier had preached duty, honor, country while this man Stephan . . .

Maishe found his car. He realized he was leaning against it for support. He fairly panted breathing hard. He suddenly knew he was shaking all over. What would he do now? He could never imagine himself—he realized that, had he been weaker he would light a cigarette. He held out his hands. The shook. He had a flash of the scene in *The Maltese Falcon*, when Humphrey Bogart hurls the glass past Sidney Greenstreet, then, a moment later, gazes at his hand quivering. Maishe's hands quivered.

He had experienced and passed his self-defense training courses. He felt ready to leverage the man to ground, there on the street, and smash him. He wondered if he was himself; but he was glad he had not resorted to the violent act. That would have been too easy, and not right. He thought of his wonderful parents, how they raised him. They would not be proud. He felt right at least he had made the correct decision, of the moment. To think that this person thought he was this way and tried to . . . Or that he now knew he was capable of inflicting so much physical damage on another human being.

He glanced up. The restaurant lights, as a beacon in a dark lonely night spilled across the roadways. She still worked the counter. Well, and why not? He stood up. He felt a bit more steady. He returned to himself. He crossed the first road. He wound his way through the median. He crossed the second road. He entered the restaurant. The couple had left. He hoped they had found a way to reconcile and were now or soon would be engaged in romantic intimacy. Maishe had always been a sucker for romance.

Two young men sat at the far end of his now regular location. Tertiary Territoriality, he recalled from one of his Psychology courses. So he sat at "his" seat. He wondered if the two young men looked at him, understanding now what it meant. He did not look at them. He looked at the girl, taking in again her strange allure.

Her thin arms moved bony-gracefully, as everything she did. Her skirt came above her knees, knobby above her thin calves. She glanced at him with that horsy-buck tooth jaw and those immense intense eyes, indicating an intelligence and depth he knew she was not aware of.

He realized there was something mysterious, something of her just out of reach that he could ponder and not ever be explained, an energy exuded by her body, mind, spirit.

The two young men sat close. They leaned in to each other. They peered at him. He turned. He ignored them. Now he knew to do so.

He fairly gazed at the oddly captivating young woman, working so competently her shift, the wafting odors of frying oil and onions her seductive perfume.

He glanced at his hands. They still shook a little. Then, she was there. He sensed her presence. Suddenly, her long bony fingers grabbed his hands. They stopped shaking.

"It's OK, hon. Come back for something else?" The s in else sounded almost a whistle, an unvoiced lingua-palatal fricative unable to cloister the sibilant. Those teeth, of course. The top button of her blouse had come undone. The slight cleavage of her small breasts hung beautifully before him.

"I, uh, yes," Maishe said. He realized he stammered. He looked down. His hands were still in hers, no longer quivering, her cool hands giving comfort she somehow sensed he knew. He looked into her eyes. She removed her hands. He smiled.

Like a flash, the vivid memory played in his mind, as if he were still there.

He recalled about fifteen years previous, his parents owned and ran a small but viable dry good store at Ninth and Market Streets in Louisville. The first years were good ones, prosperous, busy, money filling the tills. On a Saturday night, closing a good day, on the way home, his father, mother, and he stopped at a Toddle House. Always he ordered a slice of chocolate ice box pie, the cream on top of the solid chocolate whip, borne by the graham cracker crust presented a unique texture that he could taste even as an old man in his hospital bed, in his recliner at home. The memories poured in twice, as the young man now in a Little Rock Toddle House, and as an old man in his home recliner the same: He missed his mother and father. It was their family event, and his heart welled up, and he was unsure whether it helped his healing or detracted it.

"It's all right, hon," the girl said. Suddenly he knew he own hands were again steady.

"Did you see that guy, that Stephan? Hear what he said to me?"

"Yes," she said.

"Did you know he was, I mean, I did not know until it, until we were . . . "

"Yes," the girl said. "I did. They're all through here in this town, especially in this area. Thy come in, spend good money. Those two over there."

He knew it. He glanced at them. They had seen the girl grab his hands. They were interested only in each other.

"I, I want to . . . what is your name?"

"Bekthesday."

"Bekthesday. Really. So unusual," Maishe said.

"Yeah. But I could never say it as a little girl. I went around saying, 'Beh, Beh-ka.' So everyone called me, calls me 'Becca.' I made it my name. I like it."

"I like it also. Becca," Maishe said.

"Yeah. I never heard it said like that before. So dis, dist—"

"Distinct? Every consonant and vowel uttered precisely? Becca."

"Yeah," Becca said. You talk, I like the way you talk. No one I ever knew—anyway, can I get you something else?"

"Yes, Becca. A slice of chocolate ice box pie," Maishe said.

"You bet," Becca said.

"And . . ."

"Yeah?" She stopped. She turned back to him. That boney graceful move.

"What time do you get off?"

"Two o'clock," Becca said.

Maishe looked at the wall clock. It read 1:23. 0123, he thought reflexively. "OK. I could wait. I mean, that is, if you . . . "

"You have a car?"

"Yes, Maishe said.

"I always have to walk home in the dark. Takes me a while. It's not that far in a car."

"I'll bring my car around at 1400, that is at 2:00. I'll wait for you, right there in front."

"I'll get your pie and coffee. I know you want another cup of coffee," Becca said.

Maishe realized he was suddenly relaxed. The only quiver he felt now was his manhood rising. He could not take his eyes off of Becca.

She seemed smaller in the passenger seat of his car, his white Chevy II with red interior. It was his first new car. So far it ran well. Now she seemed slight, well, even more so. Still, he stole an occasional glance as he drove, according to her directions. She hadn't bothered to pull down her skirt. Her thin thighs as everything else about her strangely alluring, compelling, seductive. Her hair still hung unkempt from the faux gold clasp. She had one of those small black purses with a flap, carried by a long thin strap across her shoulder, wherein the strap crossed right at the division of her décolletage. When she entered the car, she removed the purse, deftly lifting the strap above her head with the now unkempt hair. She placed it in the middle of the bench seat, between them. For the most part, she looked straight ahead, guiding his turns. She smelled of fries and onions. He knew she would, of course. To him, seduced and besotted at the moment, it was pleasant as perfume.

Quite soon as they quit the street in front of the restaurant, one of the wide roadways of the median, they turned right on a numbered street. They crossed a busy artery. Soon, at an angle, they turned down a narrow road, one Maishe had never known was there. It was rutted, neglected.

The houses seemed neglected as well. Some held boards at severe angles over where windows should be. A couple of houses had curtains tied in a knot, hanging in the window. Here a sofa, torn, the stuffing and springs protruding graced a yard where nothing seemed to grow. There an old rusty bicycle lay in a grotesque angle. Cars with flat tires. Other things. Then he smelled it, the semi-sweet, almost cadaverous scent of poverty.

This was Becca's neighborhood.

"Here. This my house."

"You live in a house?"

"Basement apartment. My sister and her no good husband and bratty kids. They all probably asleep now. Smokin' and drinkin' themselves to sleep. And the kids collapsing by now in front the TV."

"I am sorry," Maishe said.

"Nah. It's nothing," Becca said. "You ain't tell me your name. I tol' you mine."

"Yes, Becca. You did. And I like it very much."

"Well?"

"Maishe."

"Mai-s?" The slight whistle through the teeth of the unvoiced lingua dental fricative, the sibilant 's.'

"Mai-sh."

"Mai-s."

Maishe laughed. Becca laughed. Suddenly he noted she was pretty. If she had dental work he thought she might be beautiful.

"Close enough," Maishe said.

"Well, all right. I gots to go in now. Mai-s. I'm glad you turned out not be like that Stephan. Them others. Seems wrong somehow. Yet seems like everyone needs someone. I don't know. I'm just glad you is, well, you know."

"Me too," Maishe said. "Me too."

"Yeah. You is different. Well, thanks for the ride."

She opened the door. The dome light of the car lit. It illuminated the backs of her thighs as her skirt caught up. She gave a coquettish turn of the head that all women—pubescents, teens, young adults, middle aged, the growing old, the poor, the wealthy—all know.

She ran across the yard to the door below the stoop, still facing the street. She fumbled for her key. She opened the door. She turned on a light. She entered.

He started to pull out. He glanced over. She had left the door open.

He gazed at the open door. Light spilled out, another beacon beckoning him. After a minute, he turned off the engine. He exited the car. He walked across the yard to the door. He felt rocks underfoot. From the street, a unique sound he thought he knew stopped his advance. He turned. A rusty red-brown pickup truck, clearly with a thrown rod rattled by. Even under the dim streetlight he saw the driver wore a baseball cap, backwards, a T-shirt with sleeves rolled up, a cigarette pack in the rolled up sleeve toward him. The driver seemed to glare at him. The truck rattled on down the street.

Maishe turned. He entered the apartment. He closed the door behind him.

"Back here, Mai-s," Becca called to him.

She stood at the rear of the room, clearly in front of the bathroom, just behind her, a bit to his left. An opening to his right revealed a small kitchen. The room must serve as both living space and bedroom. Perhaps she slept on the old red-pattern, frayed sofa.

The clasp now off, her hair hung longer than he had thought it might. Her tresses draped behind her and over her shoulders in front, brown cascades smelling of fries and onions, almost to her small breasts. She held a large towel in front of her. He saw she had nothing else on. For a moment he thought he would walk up to her, grab the towel away, then—but she spoke again.

"I'm going to take a bath. I'll be about twenty minutes or so. Try to get the restaurant out. Just get comfortable. Take your shoes off. And, well . . . Would you like some beer?"

"Oh. Uh, no. No," Maishe said.

"Yeah. I thought so. You is different." She started to turn. He caught a glimpse of her naked backside, boney, slight, again strangely provocative and alluring. Suddenly she turned. The towel failed to cover her right breast. Her thigh visible also for her leg was at that coquettish angle they all knew, her right foot raised against her left, her knee slightly bent, her head down slightly at a right oblique.

Maishe had an image of a ballerina he had known in his theater department.

"Mai-s."

"Yes, Becca."

"I'm sorry."

"Sorry Becca? Sorry for what?"

'I'm sorry I'm not pretty for you."

"Oh Becca," Maishe said. He could not help it. He stood close to her now. He lifted her head with both his hands.

"Becca."

"Yes, Mai-s."

"You are beautiful, in your fashion. There is nobody else on earth I would rather be with tonight."

She looked at him. Tears welled within her oversize brown eyes, glistening and twinkling gems.

"Oh Mai-s. No one ever . . . "

She smiled. For a moment he saw she was in truth beautiful or could be. He was afraid with those teeth, the fries, the onions, she might have halitosis. But no, the kiss was soft and sweet.

"I'll try to make it fifteen minutes," Becca said.

The door to the bathroom squeaked when she closed it behind her. Soon he heard the water running.

He glanced at his watch. It was getting on to 0300. And he knew that a wonderful lovely languid morning stretched before him.

The water ran. The water shut off. Then the water ran. Some more of the hot water, he supposed. He sat on the red faded frayed couch. He removed his shoes. He unbuttoned his shirt. He needed to loosen his pants, for he was ready for her and straining against the fabric.

He suddenly realized it was well into a Sunday and the feeling of despair, of depression, of dissociation was not moving in as that great gray oft-Sunday fog.

He looked across the room. The wall paper peeled. A Formica table with wooden chairs occupied the corner outside the kitchen. A small black and white TV sat on a card table across the way.

He looked around. Everything was clear, in focus.

The bathroom door squeaked as it opened.

Kendra

Spring comes early in Little Rock, in Jacksonville, and at Little Rock Air Force Base. The dogwoods bloom their multifaceted colors, fairly and of a sudden exploding in golds and reds, pinks and whites. Roses, tulips, pansies, daffodils permeate their perfumed scents through the air, on occasion overpowering with wonder even auto and bus exhausts.

Maishe continued his Saturday night excursions to Little Rock, and to Becca. Lying naked together, he told her of Greek myths and Shakespearian drama. Maishe recalled practically all of Homer's epic works Becca seemed particularly interested in Penelope's seventeen year vigil, contesting her wits with the aggressive suitors. Still, it seemed just when the facial misshapen beautiful cook-waitress gained insight, he realized she had fallen asleep. Deep asleep, her steady breathing whistled through her protruding teeth. Still, he liked to observe her small breasts rising and falling with each slow rhythmic flow of air, bringing her slight, wiry body oxygen to each of her cells, and carrying out into the ether the waste product of carbon dioxide. Everywhere we stand, sit, lay, oxygen occupies for all animal life benefit just over 20% of the unseen atmosphere. Breath is life, Maishe thought, as he watched this unique woman lying next to him, inhaling the life-giving element, even in this lower depth.

Invariably the whistling intensified. It was enough. Softly he moved her thin muscular arm laying on his chest, and, as quiet as he could, dressed, and quit the basement apartment. Thankful his car started right away, he drove to the restaurant. He ate a good breakfast—orange juice, scrambled eggs, with onion, well done, whole wheat toast and melted butter. The griddle cook was a man, about thirty, gaunt, as they all seemed to be, he competent and courteous with his multitudinous tasks. It was 0530 when he entered his own apartment. He knew he would sleep past noon, grateful for it, for the fog of lonely despair would not this Sunday creep in.

Just before sleep captured him, and, upon awakening, thence he knew the truth of the matter.

Indeed, soon she did not answer his calls, nor did she call him. He had two weekend duty tours. The first was scheduled. He survived it. He would be free the next weekend.

Then, on Friday afternoon, his phone rang. He had heard the news. He sat near the phone, waiting for the inevitable call.

"Captain Rosstein?"

'Yes.'

"It's Sanders at Documents Control."

"I know. Hi Mitch."

"Hi Maishe. You heard of the B-52 crash in Greenland."

"Yes."

"Colonel wants everyone to report here 1700. Distribution of documents and firearms at 1715. Briefing 1720. All vehicles depart at 1730."

"Understood. See you within the hour," Maishe said.

"Copy that."

He called her before he changed to his combat fatigues and boots. He tried her again at 1640 before he left to help alleviate the national crisis of the possible compromise of the nuclear launch codes.

The phone rang. No answer.

He knew the truth of the matter. He knew it as he entered the top secret rooms. He knew it as he buckled around his waist the .38 caliber firearm assigned him. He and his boss from the Trainer cross-checked the document packages assigned them. He knew it then. He knew it as they drove in the marked car through the Arkansas evening and night to Complexes 7, 8, 9. He wondered if the falcon flew overhead, seeking prey even at dusk. They drove up to the complex gate. They picked up the phone by the gate. The Commander on duty answered immediately. They gave the code word. A buzz and a click. They opened the gate. They entered the complex. As had for some time become his habit, he peered at the huge brown hillock blast doors covering the ballistic death machine below them. They opened the hidden coded door. They descended the 4 flights of stairs to the nether regions. They pressed the hydraulic charging switch to open the first of the 2 feet thick blast doors. They waited between the doors. One closed slowly, before the other slowly opened. Then the familiar hallway. He was in the Titan II missile complex Control Center again. The enlisted men were sent upstairs. The 4 officers exchanged the documents, Maishe's team noting the previous had not been opened; they handed the Commander and Deputy Commander on duty the now current documents containing the launch codes. The Commander and Deputy verified they had not been opened. They collected the signatures. They left.

So it went for the 3 complexes of their assignment. By Air Force and Sac Regulation, the complexes must be at least 25 miles separate. On they drove through the Arkansas night, perhaps the falcon following them above, repeating the proper procedure. As they returned to base, Maishe felt the nation safe again, and he, no small part in securing it. Once, outside the car window, in a farmer's field no doubt, he thought he saw a Continental Army soldier, with musket, saluting him.

The following week, when he drove into town, he immediately went to her house.

The rusty pickup was parked in front of the building. Even before he drove to the restaurant, he knew she wasn't there.

He suddenly knew he was hungry, starved. He rarely got that hungry. Now he felt it.

The cook-waitress was an older woman, avoirdupois creeping upon her at her age. Another young man sat next to him. This man tried to open that same soft conversation with its secret signals of words and finger tapping. Maishe ignored him. He moved away. He managed to sit in what he felt was his stool. He ate his meal. He finished his meal. He paid his tab. He drove back up the freeway to his apartment.

He knew he would not see her again. She had so much to offer. With some dental work and her intelligence, she could . . .but she was with . . . and in that cyclical malaise morass of poverty.

He slipped into a troubled slumber.

A chase dream: Like Mary Shelley's nightmares, an amorphous monster chased him through a cemetery, then suddenly a steep snow packed mountain, then a burst of thunder, lightening, and rain. At the top of a cliff, an aerie, an eagle's nest, a chick bursting through the egg. The monster upon him. He leapt into the darkness. He awoke in sweat.

"Well, after all," Maishe thought, wiping the cold perspiration from his head and neck. "It really was a dark and stormy night when she wrote the iconic doctor's creation."

Then he felt it. The fog crept in.

Well, the day would go by as it always did. Tomorrow he would be at his work station, and the fog would dissipate as always. He'd get a late pizza. The shop was open till 11:00. Deep into night and early morning he knew he would feel better. It was his late morning shift. He could sleep in a bit. He dressed in his home T-Shirt and sweat pants.

He used to watch the Yankees' games. He liked the players—Bauer, Kubrek, Mantle, Maris, Berra, Ford . . . And he liked Dizzy Dean's and Pee Wee Reese's broadcast. "He slood into third base, " Dean intoned. Maishe and his mother watched the Sunday games together, while his father read the paper and Whitey, their dog, moved to each for her petting.

Maybe there was a game on this afternoon. It could get him through the rest of the day after all. He began to turn on the TV.

The doorbell rang.

He gazed at the door. Curiosity consumed him. Who could it be?

He rose. He walked to the door. He opened the door.

She stood there, with a somewhat thick folder in her arms, they covered by the sleeves of her blue suit jacket. A white blouse, and a broach complimented the business attire. Blonde, blue eyes, about 5'6", although he saw she wore pumps. A red ribbon bow tie at the neck topped off the cosmopolitan outfit. The day had clearly worn on her; the blouse and jacket were now a bit too tight, probably from tension and sweat, the hair no longer perfectly coiffed, with a strand hanging down here and there. Her breasts pressed through the blouse. The blue skirt rose a bit above the knees. The sheer hose remained mostly unwrinkled.

"Yes?"

"Mr. Rosstein?"

"Captain. Yes."

"Oh. Wow. Caption. Hi, I'm selling magazines to pay my way through college. May I come in?"

Maishe knew he could on occasion be naïve and culpable. But this story he knew at once. Clearly the company engaged pretty young women to go to apartment homes, look at the names in the mailboxes and instruct the girls to find single men's names. Easy pigeons for blond or brunette or amber haired beauties.

"You may come in; but I am not interested in—well, I mean . . ." Maishe could be honest to the fault of losing opportunity. "That is, Miss . . . "

"Adams. Kendra. Kendra Adams. But you—please, call me Kendra."

"Kendra. Unusual. Well, here it is." She was beautiful. That alluring smile! That blouse! Those legs! That lilting voice, even late in the day. And those eyes, those eyes!

She moved with grace and somehow seemed already to belong in his domicile. As she entered close to him, her perfume's last dregs wafted with her fully feminine cachet permeating completely his senses. He recognized the scent at once. Lilac. He had dated a girl in high school, a cheerleader from another school. They made out in the front seat of his car in the driveway of her house, after a night out. Her scent stayed with him for days.

"Missy."

"Kendra," Kendra said.

"Yes," Maishe said. I know. You said—

"You called me Missy. It's Kendra."

"I did? I, I don't'—"

"You're kind of funny," Kendra said. Is that a mattress on the floor? Is that where you sleep?"

"Sometimes," Maishe said. "Sometimes I just fall asleep reading or just thinking."

"Yeah," Kendra said. "You work and come home tired and after dinner, you just crash."

"Yes, something like that," Maishe said. "I'm tired," Kendra said. "I've been walking around lugging these stupid samples place to place. Would you like to see some?"

"Not now," Maishe said. "Would you like some water—or coke. I have Coke."

"I don't know. Maybe. Do you think I could rest on your mattress? I'm so tired.

"Well, yes. If you—"

"Thanks," Kendra said. She sat vainly trying to keep her skirt from rising up. "Oh, look at this large pillow. I'm so tired. I've been walking all day. My feet hurt. Do you mind if I take off my shoes? I need to lie down. Only for a minute, I promise. I don't want to usurp your couch, I mean mattr—"

Usurp, Maishe thought. Fascinating word, and used properly. Almost at once he recognized the slow rhythmic breathing of a woman asleep. At least her steady sleep breathing absence of whistling.. He went to the bedroom in the rear of the apartment. He opened the closet. He reached up to the top shelf. He retrieved the extra blanket. It was blue. Perfect. He carried the blanket into the front room. He spread it, to cover her. For a moment, he thought of lifting her skirt even higher for a fuller view of her charms, her thighs, and her wondrous treasure. No. He would be an impeccable gentleman. He thought his parents would be proud.

He covered her. She snuggled under as people do when they fall asleep uncovered and there is someone about thoughtful and caring to cover them.

He watched her. She was peaceful and beautiful. He picked up the Sunday paper. He wouldn't be watching TV this afternoon after all. He turned out the light in the front room. He went into the rear bedroom.

He realized his fog had already begun to lift.

Two hours later, he heard her stirring. He walked into the front room. She sat up. Her skirt rode well above her knees. She was indeed beautiful everywhere. He caught a glimpse of the tops of her pantyhose. He felt himself stirring. Her hair lay askew. Maishe observed her brunette roots.

"Wha—what time . . . "

"Five. A little after," Maishe said.

"God. Five. After. My mother will kill me."

Kendra brushed her hair back. Instantly it fell over her eyes and brow again. An image flashed unto Maishe of one of his favorite actresses, Veronica Lake, especially thinking of her particularly astute performance in Sullivan's Travels, with Joel McCrea.

"My shoulder hurts," Kendra said.

"I think your jacket and blouse, I mean, I wanted to loosen things up for you, but, well, it might seem, appear unseemly, that is to say, as if I were, you know . . . "

"You're a sweet boy, hon. Mach, Mek—"

"Maishe."

"Maishe. And I think you said my name was unusual."

"It's a variant of Moshe, which is Hebrew. Moses. My great uncle's name. He died a month before I was born—I, I am a terrible host. Here, let me get you some water."

She coughed. He entered the kitchen. He took a glass. He poured water. He brought the glass of water to her. She was putting on her shoes. She stood up.

"Here," Maishe said.

He handed her the glass of water.

She drank, all at once, then licked her lips. She handed him the empty glass. He put it on the coffee table next to the mattress.

"Thanks," Kendra said. I needed that.

They laughed.

"I don't suppose you'd want to buy a magazine subscription."

"No," Maishe said.

"Of course not. Nobody does. That's it. I quit. Captain, huh? You're at the base?"

"Yes."

"What do you—oh, right, you probably can't tell me."

"Not very much of it," Maishe said.

"Well, thanks. I've, I should go."

"I know," Maishe said.

Again she passed close to him as she reached the front door. He started to open it. Then he closed it.

"Kendra."

"Yes, Maishe."

"This will sound, I mean, I know it's just this afternoon, but, well . . . May I kiss you goodbye? Just a short—"

She did not hesitate. Her lips were upon his ere he completed his sentence. It was sudden and suddenly wondrous. He pulled her to him. Nay, not short. The kiss long, lingering, mouth and tongues searching each other, slight mystic moans. Oh, that perfume mixed with full natural female sleep-sweat cachet and pheromone.

"Maishe," Kendra said, finally breaking, whispering in his ear, breathing hard.

"Yes, Kendra."

"I, I hope I, I mean, the moment and all . . . "

"Kendra, would you like to have dinner with me tonight? We could order in pizza. The shop down the street is open late."

"I'll have to call my mother, make up some story about a stupid magazine sales meeting. May I use your phone?"

"Of course," Maishe said.

Sleep began to wear off. Maybe the kiss helped. She moved with that natural grace again.

Maishe noticed she was removing the red ribbon as she gave the lie over the phone. She hung up. She removed her jacket. Then, she began to unbutton her blouse.

Skip

His name eponymous: Skip Lensman--photographer and filmmaker extraordinaire. A professional filmmaker, so high level, from his house-studio in Little Rock, he made local and national commercials, trailers, industrial films, slide shows for exhibitors, weddings, bar mitzvahs, anniversaries, portraits. Part of his house held a museum of old cameras, the original Kodaks, dating to 1895. It was a valuable collection. Friends of his knowledgeable of history sardonically claimed he helped Edison and Edison's man William Dickson invent the kinectoscope.

Skip Lensman was old when Maishe met him, still working well at his craft.

For some time Maishe had been interested in photography and filmmaking. He had read thoroughly, and, on his own, came to an understanding of Directional Continuity, the 2s (two-shot), spov or opov, and other cinematographic techniques. But Skip allowed him to see these and practical methods on location.

From the day they met at the camera shop, the old man and young man recognized their kindred spirit.

That is how, on the days of the weeks he worked night shift, and free from intelligence calls, Maishe Rosstein served a valuable apprenticeship with Filmtone Productions, 35mm and 16mm film production company.

This apprenticeship served Maishe well later in his academic career. Along with his later Bachelors, Masters, and Doctorate in Speech and Theater, the professional filmmaking experience and training in film history would promote him into significant faculty and administrative positions of high rank and fast track promotions.

So the days of scouting locations, loading cameras, testing light intensity for the F Stop (speeds were always 24 fps of course) coaching actors for the 30 second or 1 minute run time (whole day or two spent of the shoot), passed in joy and learning experience. The weeks he was not working nights, there were nights at Skip's house studio, for processing post production editing.

In his studio, Skip's wall clock ran backwards, cameras and cans of film perched on top of one another half-hazardly, and his large gnarly hands, still supple at his age, expertly picked and threaded exactly his need for that day.

His long-suffering wife and full partner in the business ("Lily is the best editor in the business," Skip said. Maishe, viewing the finished work, believed it).

Maishe had emergency duty the night Skip collapsed on set, doing what he always loved. But he never forgot him. And this memoir, a romance of course, is partially dedicated to him.

It was Maishe's film school, after all. Maishe had played Horatio once, in a Shakespeare summer stock company of repertoire. Horatio's line washed over his mind: "He was a man, for all that."

VII

Elizabeth

In that miasma moment in recovery, when he realized that during the full and complete blackness he had lived fully again the hours of his young adult days, he later realized he couldn't recall how he met her.

There they were though, driving north though the Arkansas countryside, to an Ozark Mountain Bluegrass Music Festival and Fair.

He had called for her at the agreed upon moment. She was punctual. She was a bit saftik, a full figured woman, as the saying goes, so he didn't think of her as particularly athletic. But she bounded down the three tier steps of her duplex apartment, with full grace. A gazelle, Maishe thought, analyzing the bounce in her step, viewing the gift of the view above her knees as the hem of her soft, flowing flowery print dress flounced.

There they were, driving north through the two lane tree and agricultural laced verdant Arkansas countryside, rising higher toward some foothills of the mountains. The waters in the streams glistened, clear, the trees towered above them, pine mostly, then as they rode higher in the hills, turned scrubbier, the air a mix of flower fragrance and occasional skunk effusion, the sun dancing in and out beyond the clouds.

"Elizabeth."

"Yes,"

"Do they call you Beth, or Liz? Some Elizabeths are called . . .

"No!. It's Elizabeth. I like it that way."

"Great. Elizabeth."

"But you have a strange name. Mash—I mean, Maishe, right?"

"That's right," Maishe said. She had a sing-song lilt in her most feminine voice that enticed men he was sure, alluring, compelling, seductive. Maishe for a moment thought of the sirens that sang alluring songs calling ancient mariners to crash upon the shoals and the wily ship's captain Odysseus saved his men and his ship. For his part, Maishe realized he would not mind succumbing to Elizabeth's charms. An unending exercise in futility, she pulled the hem of her skirt down over her knees; always it rode nearly halfway up her thighs. She was bare-legged, after her clean white tennis shoes and white cotton socks. Dark complexion everywhere, her brunette hair straight over either side of her head. Light brown eyes, so light an enchanting contrast to her complexion and multitudes of freckles. Freckles on her cheeks, as beauty mark accents, on her bare arms, and her thighs when he could catch a glimpse. Well, he did have to watch the road after all.

He drove.

One less attuned to true female beauty, their charms, their scents, their smiles, their eyes (those eyes!) might think her plump and plain. But he knew better, and hoped to see the beauty beneath her clothes, the warmth of her clearly charming personality. He found himself pondering if she had freckles . . .

"You look lovely today, Elizabeth," Maishe said, straightening out after a curve. "Beautiful in your smart outfit."

Even through her dark complexion, she blushed. Everywhere. Little rosettes played along her left thigh just above the kneecap. Interesting that unlike most women, she never crossed her legs.

"Thank you," Elizabeth said. No one—no, never mind."

And she looked at him in that particular glance women have for men they suddenly realize he is different, perhaps even compelling. Her lips pursed. She breathed a bit shallower. Could she be already thinking she might later submit? Or even dominate? As if drawn, she leaned in a bit toward him.

"You are welcome. For the truth." Then he caught the fragrance of her perfume. He knew he was already besotted.

There they were, passing a Titan II missile silo. To those who were passing, as he passenger, it seemed a large brown mound in the distance, an especial hillock of dirt perhaps. The security fence could not fully be seen. Maishe knew that below that mound of immense cover doors that could be at any moment blown apart to open, to reveal the monster lurking below, the rock thrown, the spear tossed, the atlatl projected, the arrow sent, the bullet fired, the culmination of the deadliest weapon system devised, a rocket waiting to be propelled upward into the stratosphere, to disgorge in space its ten megaton re-entry vehicle of death, wherein it would , as the demonic fallen angels, re-enter the world at its planned place of Death's own installment of utter destruction.

The Arkansas countryside of brush and farmland and streams and trees, flowers and grasses flowed by seemingly endless, strangely peaceful around Death's Door.

In the distance he saw the flash of wing he had been fortunate to observe from the open door of the helicopter, joining for his 26 hour shift or returning from it, perhaps to hunt at this very site off to his left.

"What was—what is that?" Elizabeth asked. Oh that wispy lovely sing-song voice!

"You saw it, the flash of gray-white tipped wing?"

"Yes," Elizabeth said. "What—"

"Peregrine. Peregrine falcon. Lot of rodents and small animals up here."

"Peregrine falcon. Oh."

"Yes. He's diving now. Got his eye on prey. They can reach speeds of 60 mph when diving, sometimes more."

"Amazing. Thank you Maishe."

"You are welcome, Elizabeth."

He took in her scent. He had been able to glance at those eyes. She Woman. And he could see she was already a bit thrilled. He felt his manhood rising. He must concentrate on driving.

A secret he kept to himself. He did not tell her or anyone. Maybe he would tell her later, if they . . . Once the magnificent raptor had flown alongside his helicopter, right outside the open door. It had looked right at him, three feet away, and then dove. He glanced around at his comrades.

No one else had seen it.

There they were, arriving in the main street of the quiet mountain town, bluegrass musicians jamming, strumming their ol' banjos.

They parked. They walked the town, end to end. Booths, games, music, a cultural cornucopia. They ate a lunch of hamburgers and fries, Cole slaw, homemade potato salad. A large hay ride dray drove by, pulled by a team of large draft animals.

"Maishe."

"Yes, Elizabeth."

"This food is good."

"Pure, natural I think, homemade all of it at each food booth."
"Delicious."
"Indeed."
"Maishe."
"Yes, Elizabeth."
"Can we ride on the hayride?" Those, they looked like they were having fun."
"It's gone now. Almost. Maybe they have another, another time. Well look into it.," Maishe said.
"OK. It's so charming," Elizabeth said.
"It is. I'm glad I'm here with you," Maishe said.
"Me too."

They walked down the street, looking for the booth that sold tickets to the hay ride. On the way, a carnival booth. The old throw the baseballs, knock the milk bottles.

Maishe had been, was a good baseball player. He won a stuffed razorback for the girl who had come with him.

They continued down the street. They stopped at a jewelry booth, the glittering items designed and crafted by the woman who hawked them. She wore a red beret, and one of her necklace creations. Its facets glinted in the lowering afternoon sun.

They continued down the street. They stopped to listen to three banjo players, rifting a series of pieces.

They continued down the street.

Then they saw it, together at the same time. They looked at each other, then again at the booth.

"Hayrides. Start here. One dollar," the sign over the booth read.

They realized they had been holding hands.

"One dollar," Maishe said.
"I know," Elizabeth said.
"Each," Maishe said.
"I know," Elizabeth said.
"I think I can afford it," Maishe said.

They laughed. He was again, as always, amazed, astonished, besotted utterly at how beautiful women became when they laughed and smiled.

At that moment, he recalled Suzie, a girl he had known in high school. She visited from out of state. Always she called him. They were quickly and always heading to lovers lane, doing what young lovers did at lovers lane, doing what healthy boys and girls had always done.

She was pretty and sexy. Even then and even decades later as he recalled it in his recovering room, he remembered the intoxicating scent of her, her especial female cachet, a pheromone that lingered throughout his life when he recalled her, prompting him to recall every aspect of her wonder, her hair, her perfume, her breasts, her joi de vivre, her thin ankles and thighs. Then, one time at night, they walked near the car, waiting upon the night merely, thence he saw her as she really was against a glaring streetlamp, the mist of the evening dispersing yet focusing the yellowish light. Why she was not pretty at all. Her bone structure jutted, her teeth protrusive. In an instant, even still a boy, he realized the force of her personality had covered and masked all that harsh glaring reality, that from such inner beauty of compassion, empathy, and loving life, and loving, came the outer sense.

Years later, as he studied, performed, and taught acting for stage and screen, he realized Stanislavski, the master, had been only half right. Surely emotional truth must be realized and strived for, and often attained by the inner through the outer; but Suzie had taught him it could also be the outer from the inner. Suddenly, in this quiet mountain town, the scents of good foods, barbecue, fresh produce, hay and something he could not quite discern, he smelled again Suzie's wondrous scent and felt again her wonderful teenage body against his.

"Maishe. Maishe."

"Hmm. What?"

"What was she like?"

"What? Who?"

"The girl you are thinking of," Elizabeth said. "You went away from me. I, it, well . . . "

"No. No. It's not . . . Maishe said. He took her hand. Her arms were still bare. She hadn't yet put on the sweater she brought. He gently caressed her arms.

"I love your freckles, Elizabeth," Maishe said.

"Maishe," Elizabeth said.

"Let's buy those tickets."

"OK."

"Two tickets. Two dollars," the man at the booth said. Maishe thought him out of central casting. Blue denim coveralls, read plaid shirt, long gray-white beard, mountain twang carrying his speech.

"How long . . . "

"Last one be by about fifty minutes. The night one. Gets dark quick up here. They's ice cream booth round the corner there. Good place to wait. Ma Perkins churns it herself."

Ma Perkins' Ice Cream, Maishe thought. Really.

"How long—"

"Pertnear two hour. Times a little more. Heads out to the campground barn. Banjo guitar and the Berly Boys and Girls. Real good. Real good. Ice cream booth round the corner there for waitin.' Here be yourn tickets."

"Thanks," Maishe said.

They ambled around the corner to get some Ma Perkins Homemade and Churned Ice Cream, and wait for the wagon.

They held hands.

The ice cream was smooth as silk, the chocolate he savored deep and penetrating, cool, soothing to the digestion. It reminded him of a neighborhood ice cream parlor when he was a child. The family was Italian, and people drove for miles around for their ice cream. In the summer he and his parents went almost every week. It was a wonderful memory of his parents, as he lay an old man in his recovery room. As a young man, reliving at the moment he was glad his parents were still alive. He had some leave coming. He would go to see them. For about ten joyful days he would be home.

Home!

Elizabeth had butter pecan. He snuck glances as she licked her cone with her tongue. Interesting choice, Maishe thought. Butter Pecan was his mother's favorite. There are no coincidences, he once read by a philosopher.

The Brown Hotel sat then and occupies now the central downtown corner of Fourth and Broadway in Louisville. Once, on a Wednesday at 1313, at 1:13 PM. a man named J. A. Brown checked in Room 113. Then at 1511, 3:11 PM. A man named A. J. Brown checked in Room 311. For three days, J. A. kept getting business calls for A. J.; A. J. kept getting business calls for J. A. The Browns checked out three minutes eleven seconds apart at 1:13.06 and 1:16.05. This story was told to Maishe and the storyteller swore its veracity.

There are no coincidences, Maishe had read once by a philosopher.

The moon had come out full behind a cloud, up here in the clear mountain air, a large gold disc hanging in the art gallery of the cosmos. It seemed to Maishe he could discern the orb's so called seas. Craters.

"Maishe."

"Yes, Elizabeth."

"This is the best ice cream I ever had."

"It truly is wonderful. Why are you laughing?"

"It's not funny. I don't know," Elizabeth said.

"What."

"The girl who dipped out our ice cream. I guess she'd been doing it all day. She had ice cream smudges on her arms and face, even in her hair, kind of a rainbow of colors. More interesting than funny, I would say."

"I understand," Maishe said. "As Mr. Spock would say, "Fascinating."

"You're a Trekkie."

"You?" Maishe asked.

"Yes," Elizabeth said.

They laughed together then. They finished their ice cream. They gazed at the moon. He kissed her. They kissed for a long time, for they were young and healthy and liked each other and they were having a wonderful time.

Moon glow showered them. Fragrances of foods and flora, of her lilac or jasmine perfume, of smooth churned homemade ice cream hovered about them, penetrating their senses, fully alert now to mountain air night witchery.

A breeze blew her hair askew. Then it settled, again framing her dark freckled face.

"I'll need my sweater in a little bit," Elizabeth said.

"I'll run to the car and get it," Maishe said.

They kissed again. When they broke they noticed the other tourists stealing glances at them and smiling.

He ran to the car to retrieve her sweater.

He returned as the hay wagon pulled up. He placed her sweater over her, hugging her close. They gave the driver the tickets. They found a dip in the hay where they could be close. A few others came on board. The wagon trundled along a dirt road for about fifteen minutes, then entered a clearing next to a barn. They entered the barn.

The band had begun playing, bluegrass of course. They realized they had found a half-hidden corner under the loft.

They kissed. His hands moved up her smooth woman's legs. She did not resist, and even bent her hips up to him.

"Elizabeth."

"Yes, Maishe."

"There's a shuttle outside that will take us back to town. I noticed an old motel about ten miles down the roa—"

She breathed short warm breaths. "Yes, Maishe."

The band kept strumming as they quit the barn.

Here they come, back to town, the morning sun glistening everything brighter than it seemed the day before. They passed the way they came, the car's engine now not working as hard as it would down from the mountain.

Here they were, at her house, their clothes a day older, her hair askew, and not full falling back into its frame appearance.

They kissed goodbye. Then she bounded up the steps in that same gracile manner, her skirt flowing to show der dark freckled thighs.

She stopped on one of the steps, turned to look at him, a coquettish manner, her knee bent, her head back a bit, laughing a little.

"Maishe."

"Yes, Elizabeth."

"I had a wonderful time."

"Me too," Maishe said.

"Call me."

"I will," Maishe said.

With that inherent feminine grace she cleared the steps and entered her house.

Her scent lingered in the car. An old man recovering from the most invasive of surgeries, it returned for a moment.

VIII

Casandra

For a while, seeing Elizabeth practically every Saturday night, the dark fog of Sunday stayed at the edge of the heavenly sphere; or, more likely, it emanated from another sphere, a place where darkness reigns, a place we all hope to avoid or merely sojourn. So he made it well into Monday, returning to whatever shift he worked. Always, inevitably, working in field of high intellect and demanding concentration, he felt fine. Occasionally she came to his house on Sunday, and they spent a languid afternoon of intimacy. They still had fun together.

Then, sooner than he had hoped, he recognized the distance growing between them.

His affairs always seemed to end sooner than he had reason to hope.

For some time a thought had been growing at the back of his brain. Could it be when they recognized fully his Judaism important to him, fully committed, they went searching for boyfriends of their own faith, hoping to marry and have a family.

The inevitable occurred. He knew when he dialed her number and she did not answer. After a few attempts, he drove by her house. Again, there she was in her unique, especial feminine quality. She bounded down the steps, gazelle like, her skirt flouncing to reveal her freckled things, only to his sense of loss, into the arms of another man. Older he. He wore a grey suit with a red tie. He opened the door of his white Cadillac for her.

It was over. He knew the creeping darkness at noon would return. He expected it. Return it did, with a vengeance.

One Sunday morning it became intolerable. He called his colleague, his friend, Roland. They had gone through missile school together. Roland was still heading to the silos two to four days every eight days or so.

Roland had been married almost a year to Casandra, a local model and a dancer, a classic tall, blonde beauty. He thought Roland quite lucky, not only for her pulchritude, but her kindness, compassion, and sense of humor. Her issues could be overlooked.

"Hello.

"Oh, uh. Casandra."

"Yes."

"It's Maishe. Maishe Rosste—

"Yes. Hi Maishe."

"Hi. Is Roland there?"

"No, he's on alert."

"Oh, I see." She must have heard the disappointment in his voice. "First day or second day?"

"First," Casandra said. "He left at . . ."

"About 5:30, Maishe said.

"I guess so," Casandra said. "I was sleeping. I only woke up about 45 minutes ago. What is it? 10:00?"

"10:15. I slept in also," Maishe said.

"Yeah." He heard her yawn. He imagined that gorgeous mouth open with parted lips, still faded red from deteriorating lipstick. "You don't—I mean, you're—"

"No. I'm not on crew. Not for a while now. I'm in the Trainer, Simulator. Training the crews, preparing them for Standboard tests and—"

"It's no use, Maishe."

"What?" Maishe asked.

"Roland tries to explain it. I don't—"

"Yes, I understand. Well, I called, that is, I thought if I bought some steaks later at that specialty store, I'd, you know, my treat, I'd bring them over and Roland would grill them . . . well, since he's away . . . "

"Why don't we go out?"

"What?" Maishe asked.

"For dinner. You and me. I can meet you at Sarah's Steak House. You know it, right? On Hamilton?"

"Yes," Maishe said. He had taken Elizabeth there once. He remembered how she cut her steak like a man, bold, then feminine again, daintily dropped a dollop of Lea and Perkins Steak Sause on each hearty bite, and smacked her lips, proclaiming, "Hmm. Mmm." Almost like her soft moan when their bodies were intertwined in bed.

"That's it, then. I'll let you buy me dinner. I don't want to--I think they open at 5:00. How does 6:00 sound?"

1800. He always translated. A habit now. "Six. Great." He knew what she was going to say. He felt the same on an otherwise empty Sunday.

"But won't Roland—"

"No. Not at all. He'll be glad his lazy wife and friend spent the evening together." She yawned again. "I almost feel like going back to bed. But I'm going to wash my hair and trim my nails." (And shave her legs and underarms, he was sure somehow). "I'll be ready at six. See ya then, Maishe."

As he hung up, he imagined her large bone beautiful dancer's body, as she washed her hair, fixed her nails, and all the other body maintenance. He smiled, picturing it all.

She would paint her toenails too, he knew she would, and he spent a considerable time that Sunday morn imaging that long lanky female body, her small but perfect perky breasts, long well proportioned arms, legs going on for more than any person's should. And her smile and laugh, easily producing with gleaming glistening pale blue eyes, revealing awareness of her gifts of beauty. She should be in New York or LA, Maishe realized, not in Little Rock, Arkansas; then perhaps so should he. Suddenly Maishe Rosstein understood he was infatuated with his friend's, well, colleague's really, wife. It must have been a whirlwind romance. They lived in a great high rise apartment just off the junction of I-40 and I-35.

Only a couple of years later there they would host a moon party and watch, ". . . one giant leap for mankind" live on Roland's and Cassandra's 24 inch black and white. Well, he had some time before his dinner with a charming, intelligent, and beautiful woman. He would clean his apartment a bit, maybe write a bit, one of his stories he always seemed to be writing, and get ready: Shave, Shower, dress. He would wear the blue cotton button dress shirt with white buttons, tan slacks. His best civilian clothes.

He shaved carefully, completely. He brushed his teeth thoroughly, completely. He lingered in the shower. He reached for the cologne he remembered her saying once she liked in a friendly hug. What was he doing? Was not Roland his colleague, his friend? And he down in the silo he knew so well, on alert against enemies of our nation. Still, images of Casandra crossed his mind all day; he couldn't help himself.

He suddenly knew the thick gray and black fog all too often transpired into his mind on lonely Sundays was at bay, outside. Indeed, he parted the curtain of his picture window and saw it there, a heaving, billowing, crystalline thing. Wind stirred the blue chlorine laced water of the swimming pool. A young man and woman played the waters, with her inevitable girlish screams and laughter carrying across the waves. He noted around the complex a few curtains opened just enough for the residents to follow the water games of the couple, now splashing each other, now intimate, now chasing. Iconic they were; he wished them joy and love and laughter. The breeze blew some dead leaves off the nearby trees into the pool. The leaves floated.

For a fleeting moment he thought he was like Peer Gynt, yearning just ahead of the great fog, inevitably chasing him. Today, he felt certain it would not overtake him.

Throughout the day he kept looking directly and furtively at his telephone, hoping TS Crypto did not call with a crisis. He would need to call in when he left for the restaurant to let them know where he could be reached. And, maybe from Roland and Cassandra's place later. No, Roland was deep underground 65 miles away, defending the country. It would not be right to—God, she was so lovely!

Throughout his brief affairs with fascinating young women during his tour of duty, they had all fascinated him. He had loved them in his fashion. He loved the vision and the taste and the joy of them, of their physical selves, of their unique personalities, of their intelligence. Each was a wonder, a gift to the world.

When Casandra walked in the restaurant that evening, floating that tall blond body on long dancer's legs, a vision of beauty, grace, joy, inevitably men and some women's heads turned.

"Hi Maishe."

That smile. The slight turn of the head. The mascara framed glittering blue-green eyes.

"Hi Casandra."

Well, it was all over. He knew he was done for. Poor Roland, on alert deep underground 60 miles away. Her perfume catching her own natural female scent, wafted into his nostrils. He was lost. Hopeless.

She exuded sensuality. She relished every morsel of her medium rare sirloin. The animal part of her chewed each bite as a huntress on the prowl, devouring her prey, slowly though, enjoying thoroughly the pronounced taste of this fine steakhouse fare.

"Delicious. Thank you. And these potatoes."

"My pleasure, Casandra. My pleasure." His own filet mignon came medium well, as he had ordered. It cleared his palate well and melted in his mouth at the same time.

They spoke of their dreams, when service to the Air Force ended. They discovered they both wanted to seek their dance and acting careers in Los Angeles.

She waited for him to pay the check; before they quit the establishment she said what he knew all along would come.

"I love him, I do, but marriage is hard, it's lifting weights all the time. I didn't think I'd be alone so much. Missile alert. Damn it. You don't have to do that any more, right?"

"No," Maishe said. "I mean, right." He thought ahead as he always did, as he would the rest of his life, of the things he could talk about, and the things he could never reveal.

"Right," Casandra said. She pouted. She looked around. "Let's go into the bar. I want one more glass of wine."

"Of course," Maishe said.

When she sat on the stool, it seemed she almost purposefully let her skirt ride up. She held up her glass to his. "To us," Casandra said.

"To us," Maishe said. Their glasses clinked. They drank.

"Tonight," Casandra whispered, in a huskier voice.

"Tonight," Maishe said. Lost. Hopeless.

"Maishe."

"Casandra."

"Could you stay with me tonight?"

He started to say, "But Roland . . . " He thought better of it. He downed his drink. He thought when he answered her, he might choke on the word. But somehow it emerged clear, strong.

"Yes!

Whether she ever told Roland of that night or not he never knew. They seemed to settle into the old collegial relationship.

Hearts

Sometime after Aldrin's step-leap upon the planet orbiting our own, Roland and Casandra separated. He later learned she had begun abusing drugs and alcohol. He recalled that night when she kept wanting another drink.

After he separated from the Air Force, he never heard from either of them again. He heard they had divorced.

IX

Eugenia

"She's an old woman, must be in her 80's, old Little Rock, you know. 84, 85 maybe. But still sharp as a tack."

It was a week Maishe had his night shift in the Trainer. He worked these days with Skip Lenson. Lenson had taught him a film school training level in cinematography.

"She'd like some photographs of her garden. It is magnificent really. You know, I haven't done stills for a long time. Well you know, we do those slide shows and film strips for conferences and businesses; but I don't do private. I know you have some good equipment and take excellent stills. I think you'll hit it off with her. You like old people, like me and Maurine."

They laughed. Maurine was Skip's long suffering wife. Somehow she kept "her" kitchen and living area of their home neat, in contrast to Skip's work areas.

Maishe's first solo assignment.

With some twists and turns he found the narrow street, avoided the potholes, as if time and the city had forgotten this old area of town.

The house sat at the end of the dead-end street, an old clapboard from the 1920's, maybe even earlier. A feature that struck Maishe was the full wrap-around porch, with a glider swing-sofa, and room for a small table and delicate chairs. Maybe the house dated to the late 19th century after all. He imagined people out of a summer's eve, walking about, strolling, visiting each other on the welcoming and inviting verandas, dressed up fine in suits and flowing gowns. Oddly, the old-timey song, "Daisy, Daisy," came to him. He began to hum it, then tried to think of the lyrics, and was only partially successful. "Daisy, Daisy, are you my darling dear . . . Will you, could you . . ."

No, that wasn't it exactly. He would research it later, as he always did (those days, by going to the card catalog in the library, truly a wonderful way to search, even if fully passe at the writing of this romance, of course).*

> *Daisy, Daisy, by Harry Dacre 1892
> Daisy, Daisy
> Give me your answer do!
> I'm half crazy
> All for the love of you!
> It won't be a stylish marriage,
> I can't afford a carriage
> But you'll look sweet upon the seat
> Of a bicycle made for two.

Maishe imagined men and women on bicycles. He read a treatise that it was the bicycle that had contributed to the new-found freedom and independence of women. One simply could not sit, pedal, steer with complex brocades and hooks and petticoats, nor certainly the ludicrous and demeaning side-saddle manner of horseback riding. So it was the Gibson Girl gained her profile that served as precursor to the more intense feminism of the modernist and contemporary periods. She could do very well on her own on her bicycle, thank you very much, and, for that matter, in growing professions as nursing. Why, not all that much in the future, she could even vote!

However it all came about, Maishe was glad, thankful. He loved women. He regarded them always as equals. He desired them as equals. In their fierce beauty matched by their high intellect, clearly they were the superior gender. Well, sometimes.

The stairs creaked as he walked up to the porch, to the front door. He began to wonder about his assignment. The walkway path leading up to the steps was practically overgrown with fecund weeds, covering what seemed like gallant but losing the battle rows of pansies, straining for the sun. Indeed the medium sized front yard filled in lush fervent kind. Still, a flowing, blossoming mimosa stood proud sentinel.

There was no bell button he could find. He knocked on the door. His camera bag shifted. He pulled it up over his shoulder. He waited.

He heard the gnat buzzing to his ear; as always too late, his attempt to swat it failed. A few birds chirped. An old man with a cane shuffled to the dead end, turned, and shuffled back up the street. He stopped. He coughed. He spat. He pulled out a red-checkered kerchief, coughed again. He stood there for a moment, still, still as the mimosa it seemed, for there was no breeze to shake its leaves. Perhaps he had strolled this street as a young man, and he was, for a moment, recalling his youth, and all the friendly neighbors, now moved away, or gone. It is a wonderful thing to be young, Maishe thought, to have one's life before him or her, and the days opening as a wide meadow of pretty flowers. The old man put his cane to sidewalk. He shuffled up the street.

The door lock slipped. The door creaked open. He realized she had been looking at him through the tight drawn curtain. She opened the door. She stood before him.

She was small, slightly built, but she had all her gray hair, pulled back in a bun, as she had probably done her whole life. Her eyes, steel-blue, peered in a clear, non-hazy truth. He noted her voice was strong; it did not crack, as a gammer's might.

"You're the young man Mr. Lenson sent?"

"Maishe Rosstein, Miss Carstairs."

"Oh heavens, none of that. Eugenia."

"Eugenia. Then, Maishe."

"Maishe," Eugenia said, right the first time, which wasn't always the case. "Well don't stand on ceremony or my porch. Come on in, young man. Maishe."

He shifted his bag. He entered the house. The wooden floor creaked.

"The garden's in the back. I want some nice pictures to leave my nieces and nephews. If you hadn't noticed, I am old now. When one attains my age, one never knows when—well, I guess no one does in any case."

"Well, Mis—Eugenia, I—"

"The bother. It's all right. Everyone gets old and dies eventually. There was speech about that in a play I wrote once. Well, I wrote many things. I was invited to New York back in—oh, let's see, Roosevelt had just—I suppose, now that's Teddy you know. Maybe I was 25, full of something of myself. I showed my work to a professor. He knew a producer in New York, if you can imagine. Invited me to read it. Maybe . . . "

Here she paused. Maishe noticed the eyes were not as piercing.

"My father would not let me go. Thought his daughter should only learn to take care of the house. Hid the man's letter from me. Hausten. James Hausten. I remember it to this day. I just thought like so many theatre managers he was not interested. I found it years later. Who knows what—what . . . "

It was clear to Maishe that, like so many of us, a wrong decision early in life, one ponders what might have been practically every day. Eugenia Trivoli obviously did.

"I'm sorry Ms. Car—Eugenia."

"Oh bother. In my house for two minutes and I'm, here, this is the way. Maishe, isn't it?"

The sparkle had returned to her eyes. Clearly she had adjusted to her life through the years. "Yes."

"You're a photographer, a filmmaker, and, I'll make a wager, six to one even, you're a writer."

"I, yes, I do write," Maishe said. How . . . "

"Well now. Do you know where that line came from, six to one even?"

"*The Maltese Falcon*. Humphrey Bogart."

"Wonderful. A young person who knows the great films, the old great movies. How did you—"

"Late night classic movies on a local station," Maishe said. "I have a touch of insomnia."

"Yes, yes, me too," Eugenia said.

Here she paused again. Maishe knew already she was thinking of a time long ago.

"You ever see Charlie?" she asked.

"Charlie?" Maishe said. "Char—oh you mean Chaplin. Yes. The Kid. City Lights. Amazing films. Amazing talent."

"I'm so glad Mr. Lenson sent you, Maishe. Young people have no idea. He was so big, you know. We didn't say, 'Let's go to a movie. We'd say, 'Charlie's in town. We must go see Charlie.' Yes, that's how it was. People today don't . . . "

Here another one of those pauses floated over those piercing eyes, clouding over. Maybe if he . . .

"Eugenia?"

"Yes, Maishe."

"You said you wrote a play once. I'd like to hear it. Maybe a scene anyway."

He said the right thing. Her eyes focused clear again. Teddy Roosevelt, not Franklin. She must be at or near 90.

"I know a scene by heart. Let me get you some tea or water."

"Water's fine. I'll be out in the garden much of the afternoon."

"Just a moment."

She turned. She entered the kitchen. He looked around. Photographs from ages past. A gold cabinet with glass beveled doors revealing delicate ceramic painted teapots. Other ornaments and statuettes. Clearly a lifetime of collections.

"Here you are."

He took the crystal wide glass, probably from 100 years ago. The ice tinkled.

"Here we can sit in the veranda. We can't spend too much time. You'll want to go to the back for, for the pictures."

"It's all right," Maishe said. "Often the later afternoon light is best."

"Yes, I see," Eugenia said.

The screen door slammed, bounced, and quietly closed. Funny he hadn't noticed it the first time.

"Here we are," Eugenia said. That sat at the round table he had noticed in the delicate chairs. He noticed the old man walking the street again.

"Old Mr. Cogson. Poor dear. He's got the dementia, you know."

"Should we—"

"No," Eugenia said. It's all right. His granddaughter will come get him directly. I don't think she can handle much more though. A nice young woman. But she has her job and her life too you know. I suspect they'll take him to one of those places."

"I see," Maishe said.

"Yes. Well. Ready for my little literary achievement in the dramatic arts?"

"Yes, yes indeed."

Maishe drank his water. Birds chirped. Insects buzzed. Old Mr. Cogson coughed. The ice in his glass clinked.

"Well, in essence," Eugenia started, her voice strong and breathy at the same time, occasionally cracking in the manner of the elderly, "The play is about two women who are friends, best friends since high school. Later, without knowing, they fall for the same man. He knows, that is, he strings both Emily and Sarajane along."

"Not a nice fellow," Maishe said.

"No. We used to say a cad. I believe the worst today is 'jerk.' Now, I reckon you are not a jerk, are you, Maishe?"

"No ma'am."

"No. A gentleman I'll wager. So, the time comes when Emily and Sarajane find out about this two-timer. Now Emily is a secretary in a police station. I guess today—well, doesn't matter. The point is, she has learned how investigations work. Sarajane's father tends an estate garden with pathways leading to a forest. I think you see where this is going."

"They, they plot to—"

"Yes," Eugenia said. "Do the blighter in. No man is going to make fools of these girls and get away with it. Now, here's the scene when they discuss the plan. Part of it anyway. Very well, excerpt from The Pl—But your water glass is empty. Would you like a refill?"

"I'm fine," Maishe said. "Really."

"Yes, well. Excerpt from *The Plot*."

"The Plot. Wonderful. A double entendre," Maishe said.

Then he wondered, did he see a tear cross her wrinkled cheek? "Yes Maishe. You're the first person to see that."

She paused again. He noted there was no manuscript. She said it from memory. She repeated the synopsis introduction, then went on.

"Excerpt from *The Plot*.

The scene is Sarajane's bedroom on the estate. The Forest, pine mostly is seen through the windows behind them."

Maishe could not contain himself. He interjected. "Not unlike the birch trees in Checkhov's play. Only here there are 2 women and not 3, and no men upstage."

Eugenia continued the interruption. "I saw that play once. Later I realized it was a poor translation. Translators are better today, truer to the work somehow I think. Well, all translators are traitors, you know. That's an Italian expression. Very alliterative. Works quite well in English, don't you think?"

"Yes, Maishe said.

"Ironic," Eugenia said.

"The height of irony," Maishe said.

A summer breeze, delightful, wafted into their pause. They drank their water. She looked out at the neighborhood close by but he knew she looked far, far away. Suddenly a commotion from up the street welled up. Maishe craned his neck. Poor old Mr. Congson's granddaughter tried to get him back in the house. Maishe heard the strain in the woman's voice. He thought he heard, "Nursing home." Then, suddenly as it was as before, quiet settled on the street. Then he heard the bees buzzing again, a train wailing a mournful tune in the distance.

"Ah, me," Eugenia said. A lovely afternoon. A hot summer's afternoon cool breeze is a gift."

"I'm sorry I interrupted," Maishe said.

"Well, it's all right."

"Please continue."

Eugenia had set her scene. She now continued with her dialogue.

"Sarajane
Out there.

Emily
In the woods?

Sarajane
Yes. There's a deep pit beyond that cottonwood. The roots go deep over the pit, cover it. They'll never find him.

Emily
Never say never. The police are smarter than most people think.

Sarajane
That's when you need to think like them.

Emily
They'll look everywhere. I know the spot. It might work. We picnicked there once in high school. Near there. Jay Weintrock tried to . . .

Hearts

Sarajane
Yes. I had forgotten. Whatever happened to him?

Emily
A doctor or something. He moved out of town. It might work.

Sarajane
There's an odd little cave off and under it.

Emily
Yes, I remember.

Sarajane
It angles this way and that way. A tight fit for more than one person.

Emily
If we could get him way into it . . . the entrance is hidden, isn't it?

Sarajane
Yes.

Emily
We can't shoot him. They'll be all over that.

Sarajane
Right.

Emily
Don't say 'right' again. You'll drive me crazy. I'm trying to think.

Sarajane
Righ—I mean, yes. Yes.

Emily
I read something about potassium once.

Sarajane
Poison, then.

Emily
A certain kind. Not outright poison. Something about potassium. Too much can bring on or make it look like a heart attack. Somehow it becomes undetectable. I saw it once in one of the reports.

Sarajane
Can you find it again? Find out how it—

Emily
I think so. Yes. I'll say I need to research the file for a request. I'll have to be careful though.

Sarajane
That bastard.

Emily
"Router." Emilia interrupted her reading. "I think I'll change that word to 'jerk.' What do you think, Maishe"
"Yes," Maishe said.
"So, Emilia said.

Emily
Jerk!

Sarajane
It occurs to me . . .

Emily
Yes?

Sarajane
Other women.

Emily
Other women. You mean . . .

Sarajane
We'll be doing them a great favor. And they will . . .

Together
. . . never know it.

Emily
It's beautiful out there.

Sarajane
Who could suspect?

Hearts

Emily
They will suspect. They always suspect.

Sarajane
You need to be careful.

Emily
We need to be very careful. Very.

Sarajane
You are suddenly quiet. Emily. Emily.

Emily
Yes.

Sarajane
What are you thinking about?

Emily
Death.

Sarajane
Yes, but . . .

Emily
We are born. We live. We die. Each of these is a mystery. But the greatest mystery of all is death.

Sarajane
The undiscovered country.

Emily
From whose borne no traveler returns.

Sarajane
Mr. Compton's Shakespeare section of English. You had a crush on him, didn't you?

Emily
Never mind. Enough philosophy. Let's get down to brass tacks, as Detective Carter always says when he interviews a suspect.

Sarajane
I heard something about death once.

Emily
What? Where?

Sarajane
On radio. One of those odd shows that you catch between things. Unexpected like, you know . . .

Emily
Like a melody or a song catches your fancy.

Sarajane
Yes. Like that.

Emily
Go on.

Sarajane
He was a coroner, a doctor that helped to solve mysterious deaths.

Emily
That's a bit close.

Sarajane
I know. Still . . .

Emily
It's OK. We'll be OK. Go on.

Sarajane
He said, 'We die three times.'

Emily
Three.

Sarajane
Yes. The moment our body gives out fully, and we are buried. Then, years or decades later those who buried us die and are buried and

their memories of us lost, erased. Then, last seen and heard, decades beyond those who were told of us by those who recalled us, even they die and carry with them the last remnant of our memories of who we were or might have been. Centuries pass and even our graves are grown over and we join the untold hordes of the forgotten.

> Emily
> It's, I don't . . .
>
> Sarajane
> I know.
>
> Emily
> Do you still think we should?"

At last she glanced over at Maishe. She gestured her hands into her lap, as though she had placed carefully her pages, and smoothed them out. "Well?"

"It's wonderful," Maishe said. He meant it. "I'm fully involved. I want so much to find out what happens."

"It's a terrible thing, to have good work go unknown, unnoticed, to die one's death, never fully lived."

"I know what you mean," Maishe said.

A pause ensued. Maishe heard an old clock ticking from another part of the ancient house.

"Eugenia."

"Yes.

"The afternoon light has changed. Clouds have dissipated. I should . . . "

"Come," Eugenia said. "I'll show you the garden."

Spry she was, already on her feet, down the stairs and walking around the side of the house.

"Grandpa, I mean it." Maishe thought he heard old Mr. Cogson's granddaughter yell from down the street.

He followed Eugenia around the side of the old house. They entered the backyard. He stopped, for the garden beckoned, as myriads of multi-hued flowers called forth with fragrances of glory.

The kaleidoscope colors of the flowers burst forth to greet him.

The bee buzzed about. The winged yellow and black fuzzy insect searched for the perfect nectar. He would remember the creature always, throughout his life occasionally, recalling that liminal moment when it lighted in perfect repose upon the rich red rose. His tripod at the ready, he held his breath hoping the creature remained, extracting the wondrous fluid from the plant. Only its head moved, ever so slightly, as its proboscis ingested what nature provided in harmony and symbiosis.

He set up his tripod. With care, he turned the Roliflex onto the screw. He removed the lens caps. He opened the top viewfinder of the 2 ¼ X 2 ¼ frame. He focused on this moment, a moment of Sontag's moment, a haunting moment, calling forth time itself.

For he recalled a passage he had read, that the world was young when our species appeared, and, as if they had been waiting for us to appear, did flowering plants bloom.

He focused. He aligned. He caught the composition he wanted in the sweltering Arkansas afternoon sun. He pressed the cable release. The shutter clicked. He had it! He knew he had the money shot!

For the rest of his life and e'en as an old man recovering bed, he recalled that moment in time, always so vividly, it was as if it had just occurred.

He took more pictures, many pictures, all vibrant, composed well, exuding the grandiose beauty of her magnificent garden; this he knew even prior to seeing the negatives and prints. None would be as exciting nor exacting as capturing the bee upon the rose petal.

The afternoon wore on. He had to depart. He had his night duty. But he carefully tended the two rolls of exposed color film. When enlarged from his negative size, they would blow up with little loss. He knew she would adore them.

She stood on the porch. She waved goodbye.

"I'll be in touch," Maishe said.

She smiled. She returned into her family home in the old neighborhood, the last on a dead-end street in a nearly forgotten part of town.

Down the street, old Mr. Cogson's granddaughter cajoled him into her car. She was quiet this time. This time the old man appeared complacent, resigned.

In the distance, a train whistle blew, a sound as distant and distinct, with the same wonder as Chekhov's broken string.

He returned to his apartment. He shaved. He brushed his teeth. He showered. He donned his uniform of the day. He quit his rooms, on his way to perform his duty.

Later, when he showed her the gorgeous 11 x17 color photographs he had painstakingly shot and judiciously chose from the proofs, she was thrilled. She called her friends to come over to see them.

"Maishe, you've made my life complete now. They are magnificent (they were, really). What you have done for me . . . " Maishe recalled a commentary by the rabbis, when Jacob died in Egypt. After a life of troubles and travails, a son thought lost returned, and he could bless his grandchildren. All his sons would become tribes to carry on his name and his God.

"If the end is good, it was all good," the saying of the rabbis.

She gave him more money than he believed she should. She refused to dicker. He begged out to return to duty. Only later, when he went through his pay envelope again, did he find her poem.

"Well," Skipper Lenson said. "It seems you did well for our assignment. Eugenia called me. She praised you. She asked me over. Your pictures are beautiful."

"Thank you."

"Great composition, and you placed your lens perfect for the afternoon light."

"Thanks. Really," Maishe said. His mentor was pleased. What more could be said?

"Are you free tomorrow?" Lenson asked. "We have a 30 second commercial. If we start at 9, we should be done by 4."

'Yes, that'll work," Maishe said.

The commercial was for a cleaning agent. They used stop action and double exposure to demonstrate before and after, filth magically transforming unto the pristine.

A good week had passed. Though he still feared somewhat the Sunday fog nemesis, he found himself looking forward to the weekend.

Pictures

By

Eugenia Carstairs

I had a garden

In my yard

Flowers yearning e'er

For the sun

Hidden from view

Only I could see

Their magnificence

He brought his camera

And gave birth

For all to see

For all to relish

In the view

Magnificence.

Flowers will fade

Seasons change

Some n'er seen again

But pictures capture

Time, Time

Magnificence

And in repose I can view

My red, red rose

Susan

She was the clerk at the camera store he bought his film, cameras, and equipment. She was knowledgeable. She was gracious. She was a bit plump but pretty in the way plump but not fat nor obese girls and women are. Zoftig! Ash blonde hair and blue piercing eyes, all that, would have been enough, but the kicker was her accent.

An older woman, Maishe knew, maybe pushing forty.

A married woman, Maishe found out. He knew he should not She knew she should not. Soon enough the woman of a certain age and the young Air Force officer discovered they could not help themselves.

The store was spacious, well laid out. Appropriately for camera and film shop, bright lights pervaded the various displays of high level cameras in the showcases. Hobbyists and professionals rubbed shoulders in its aisles, the conversations according expertise clear in aesthetic and technology, the art, the craft, the science of it all.

He once realized he saw Susan in photography and filmmaking conjoined, saw her flash before him in 24 frames per second, saw her in film noir, Humphry Bogart and Ingrid Bergman. Of all the camera shops in all the world, I had to walk into hers.

It began simple enough, without warning. They discussed the discipline as he considered his purchases. Then, at the cash register.

"Here you are."

That British lilt!

"London, right?" Maishe asked.

"Yes, love."

Love!

"How did you . . . ?"

It had been as much luck as his skill at voice development and speech, his voice and acting training.

"Sometimes I can get it," Maishe said. "Other times only of beautiful, charming, and intelligent British women."

For an attention starved woman whose husband seemed to have lost interest, it was as a shutter release Sontagian moment in time. A moment in which she wanted to instruct this young man in more than one way. He is young, Susan. So young, so wondrous.

A few more visits. Now he waited in the parking lot for her when she left work.

They could not help themselves.

Then, the curiosity had run its course, as sudden as it had developed. No more sneaking around in parking lots, covering her head as she made her ways to his apartment. They parted good friends, in the same parking lot they had first secretly met.

These things he always remembered: Her soft voice; Her older, softer, alluring body she at first felt embarrassed about; The scent of her lavender perfume; Those eyes; That accent.

This also he had come to know: If she was any indication, British women are great at kissing.

Rosalie

Maishe lived a double life. He performed his duty well. He pursued alluring women. He loved them, in his fashion, a time; always they seemed to leave him.

Perhaps when they found out he was Jewish, and it occurred to them that marriage would never occur.

Indeed, that was his other life: For, any Saturday morning he could, he drove down to Little Rock to the Orthodox shul, the synagogue. There was also a Reform Temple in town. But Maishe knew the traditional liturgy and felt at ease davening prayer in that service. As customary, there were the five Shabbat morning services.*

He became known, almost a regular. He came to know the rabbi, Rabbi Ataman, a most observant man, both kind and strict at the same time.

It was true he did not have much of a Friday night kiddish meal, and after services on Saturday, as often as not, he would amble the few blocks to the Corredor Hotel Coffee Shop for lunch, pleased to see Sally when she worked. Then he might take in a new movie in the theatre down the street before returning home late in the day, earlier to read his current book, if he hadn't a date. He might return to the all night restaurant at one or two in the morning.

He had been particularly enthralled with Michael Chriton's *The Andromeda Strain*. He sat down to read at six one evening, thinking he'd get up in almost 45 minutes for dinner. When he closed the book and looked up, it was 3 A.M. The same or similar phenomenon had occurred to him with James Michener's *The Source* and T. E. Lawrence's *Seven Pillars of Wisdom*.

These became his books. Compelled, intrigued, he read them over a few days. Max Dimont's *Jews, God and History* kept him similarly enthralled.

One book would forever influence his outlook on life: Desmond Morris's *The Naked Ape*.

He found he was with women less now and with his books more, when off duty. Even the Sunday fog of loneliness had dissipated. One day it simply occurred to him it was so.

Perhaps it could be traced to his double lives meeting and coalescing.

He happened to look at the calendar for the next day's date. June 4, 1967.

It was late Sunday night. It happened toward midnight. His phone rang. Required to always be within five rings, he answered in two. It did not matter. He had been expecting it for some days now. He read the newspapers. He watched television. He listened to radio. Officers and enlisted discussed it. Seven Arab nations were going to overrun Israel. It looked bad. Many thought it heralded the end of the Jewish nation state. The officer corps, especially those high in intelligence, were not so sure.

"Hello."

"Maishe?"

"Thomas?" Maishe recognized the voice of his intelligence office colleague at once.

"He wants us to report soon."

"Soon," Maishe said.

"1330."

"Soon indeed," Maishe said. "Uniform?"

"Regular summer Class A. No going out."

"See you in a half hour," Maishe said. He cradled the phone. He placed his bookmark in his book. He caressed the book as he put it down. He knew it might be a while ere he could return to its pages. He leaned forward. He cradled his head in his hands. He closed his eyes. He rested for two minutes. He arose. He shaved. He showered. He dressed. He quit his apartment. His car started. He drove to the base. The Air Policeman saluted him through. He drove around to the familiar building.

Major Stone opened the slit in the door. He closed the slit. The second door buzzed. Maishe entered.

Everyone walked into the briefing room. The long table held enough space and chairs for the twenty officers. Maishe took his customary place. Briefing materials welcomed him.

Colonel Sutter entered. The men stood in unison, at attention.

"At ease. Be seated."

The men sat in unison.

Maishe could never stop noticing the similarity the Colonel bore to the actor, Donald Pleasance. His doppelganger, really. Maishe suddenly recalled Pleasance, Stephen Boyd, and Raquel Welch in Fantastic Voyage. One of our spies (or was it one of theirs?) had suffered a stroke, and lay in a coma. But the important information held in the man's brain. Edmund O'Brien led a special team who could shrink ships and people small as blood corpuscles. The team entered his body and made its way to the brain through the special effects of lungs and heart and antibodies attacking them and . . .

The lights dimmed. Maishe pushed himself out of his reverie. Captivating as the film was, the premise was outrageous and mere fiction. Here he now concentrated on the theatre of the real.

Black and white clear images projected on the wall screen before them.

"Gentlemen, what we are seeing is the Egyptian Air Force destroyed. Utterly. Here is the Syrian Air Force. Planes and runways destroyed. All in pieces as they lay in order on their tarmacs.

"At 0545 Mid East time, a squadron of Israeli Mirage fighter-bombers flew across the Mediterranean Sea about 500 feet above the water, circled back to begin their bombing runs and fully eliminated any Arab air power. A pre-emptive strike, and a brilliant one.

"Gentlemen, I will tell you now that whatever happens in the next days and weeks, this will be fact: Israel has won the war!

It was so Air Force philosophy, Maishe thought. Air power is the ultimate weapon. Well, it was true enough if done fully and without hesitation. Still, at a conference once, an old soldier had said to him, that until the foot soldier occupies that land, that road, that hill, that building, it is not yet won.

In this case it seemed Colonel Sutter was right. Israel controlled the skies. It could bomb at will, support its ground troops indiscriminately. He always felt amazed at these remarkable pictures. Maishe knew how they had been taken.

As early as the 1950's the United States had developed airplanes of high performance jet aircraft that could fly over Mach 2, and as high as the edge of space. Two airplanes in particular—the U2 and the SR71 Blackbird would be highly classified, until one was shot down over Russia.

With a concurrent secret advance in camera shutter speed and telescopic lens technology, as early as 1959 to 1964 highly detailed photographs could be taken from VHA (Very High Altitude). This was the manner in which President John Kennedy was able to bring Nikita Khrushchev to task over the Cuban Missile Crisis. Now these remarkable detailed photographs projected before him in the Intelligence Briefing Room at the opening of The Six Day War.

Decades later, as an old man in his recovery room, Maishe knew the truth of the matter. Satellite imagery had long taken preference. The government denied its two spy planes still operated.

The pilots Maishe knew had long since retired of course. But he knew valorous men and women now regularly strapped themselves in, and flew to the edge of space in craft developed with utmost secrecy and snapped their astonishing photographs.

"I know it is late, gentlemen, and as you know the crew briefings are at 0700. I've called in a few early and they'll give the briefing in the morning. Your briefing notebooks will have your assigned days, updates every six hours or so. We'll meet every day at 1930. Questions? Dismissed."

0930, 1600, 2230. Maishe checked his binder for a quick peek. His first crew briefing was Tuesday. He could get some sleep before reporting in the morning.

He left with a certain heartfelt emotion he felt the others did not share. Well, one never knew, really. After the public news reports for days, now the true information, known only a few now, soon to be known to the world, set his heart at ease.

Israel would be safe!

On a spring morning, a month or so before the events of that historic summer in June, Maishe had risen early, and proceeded with his morning ablutions preparing for his morning shift. He happened to catch on his radio the report that the U.S absolutely denied the existence of a certain Blackbird plane that could fly at Mach 2.5, perhaps more to the very edge of space and take detailed photographs at that distance of objects on the ground.

That was the essence of the broadcast. He heard the rumors and had wondered about it. Now his bosses denied it. Probably it was being thought of, a concept, Maishe thought.

To get to this duty station the low long brick building that housed the Trainer Complex for the Titan II ICBM Combat Crews at one end and the top secret intelligence unit at the other end, he must negotiate the road about and parallel to the flight line.

This day, as he turned onto that access road, he saw it at once. There below, on the flight line, a black Valkyrie, a dark majestic flying raptor, a victory of beauty and terror at once. It was without question the SR 71, and surrounded with heavily armed Air Police. He recalled almost being awaked in the night by a strange quiet roar he could not fully distinguish.

It was a thing of beauty, of terror, a joy of glory.

He had other calls at that time, from people he had met at the synagogue, families, men and women clearly frightened; Israel would be overrun, destroyed, another holocaust. After all, how could she withstand seven Arab armies? There was a special meeting at the Reform Temple, community wide. A representative from the State was coming in. The nation state, not even twenty years in existence, needed money for its war effort, an existential war, as they all were. Surly though she would be defeated and then what?

Maishe stood silent, the only person in the room who knew the truth of the matter. The Mirages screamed over the skies, destroying the enemies' tanks, artillery, battalions. Israel's columns cut through the enemy, unimpeded toward Cairo, Damascus. Long ago Saul who became Paul had trod this road to Damascus, with a different revelation than the one in June, '67. Positive reports entered the group's meeting room that even the Old City of Jerusalem was being advanced upon. Jerusalem, for the first time in nearly 2,000 years, would be united under a Jewish government.

This and more he knew that fearful meeting night and could only listen in in silence, nod to the men and women who approached him so apprehensively. So highly classified, he could say or do nothing to assuage their fears.

Then a few days passed. It was over. The world now knew the truth. The special meetings continued, but at a lesser pace. After a week or two, all returned to normal.

But the world would never be the same. Now it was clear that the mighty men of King David had returned. This island of democracy in a sea of dictators and flawed Arab reasoning would defend itself.

Twenty-five years ago, it seemed the end of Jewry. Now not merely to survive, but power had returned.

So the days and years passed. He was still young, but he realized the days of his youth, the innocent naïve days, neared their end. He had made the transition into an adult man. It would have happened in any case. No doubt his Air Force life had accelerated it. He enjoyed having access to classified and secret information. The populace did not know how well protected our country was; probably is. He continued working for Skip Lensen when he could, learning the difficult discipline of cinematography, and at Skipper's suggestion, becoming a student of the history of cinema.

Then he met Rosalyn. Everything changed for the rest of his life.

He knew Melodie Marcus from the synagogue and her parents. Melodie had invited a girl friend from another state that weekend. As always required he answered the phone within five rings.

"Hello."

"Maishe?"

"Melodie?"

"Yes.

"Hi. Is everyth—

"Everything's fine. My parents and I were wondering if you would like to come by for Friday night dinner. If you're not working."

"Actually, I think so," Maishe said. "I'm on days this week. That's be great. Of course, you know, something could—"

"Yes," Melodie said. "It's all right. Would 7:00 do?"

"Sounds right," Maishe said.

"You remember how to get to our house?"

"I think so." They went over the directions.

When he saw her that evening, he knew at once.

They wrote letters, talked on the phone, and he drove the two hours to her home when he could get coverage to spend the weekend with her. They went to a local lake beach. They built a beautiful sand castle. By the end of the day they knew.

The married within the year, a large Orthodox wedding.

As Robert Bolt stated through Eleanor, "Every family has its ups and downs." They had theirs, but they were always there for each other.

Now, over forty years later, a wonderful son, a great daughter-in-law, three magnificent grandsons. And Rose--she was there for him in hospital.

Now, here he was at home, recovering in his recliner chair, eating Rose's chicken soup, an old man remembering his memories. He remembered his bachelor days as if it were yesterday. Then he pondered. How wonderful it was to be young, to have been young, and hope to feel young again. Then it came to him. He knew.

He had lived. He would live.

He lives.

Rose, as beautiful as she was when he saw her walk down the aisle, entered the room.

Appendix

Wherein is discussed the Jewish Liturgy, especially *the five services of Shabbat and Yom Tovim, the Sabbath Day and the Holy Days; and a selected bibliography of the History of Heart Bypass Surgery, and previous medical advances.

*Observant Jews [in orthodoxy typically only men; women, according to the Talmud (Tractate B'rachoht, Blessings) being released from time bound obligations; in other movements, as Conservative, Reform, Reconstructionist, women may and do participate fully] pray three times a day—morning, afternoon, evening. With the exception of Monday morning, Thursday morning, and Friday evening, these services are straightforward and accomplish the required number of prayers. However, on Monday morning and Thursday morning, the Torah scroll is removed from the Aharon hakodesh, the Holy Ark, and three readings of that week's Torah (Pentateuch) portion is read. On Friday evening, an additional Kabalat Shabat (Welcoming the Sabbath) service occurs. On Saturday morning and on Yom Tovim, five services (actually six, if the Rabbi's d'rash or sermon is counted) occur. They are: p'sukei d'zimrah (Introductory); shachreit (morning service, similar to the other morning services); Torah—the removal and reading of the portion of the week, this time in traditional settings, seven readings, thence an eighth, which leads to a reading selection from Prophets or other post-pentateuchal Old Testament entries related to that Torah portion. Typically the Rabbi's sermon or lesson occurs following the return of the scroll to the Ark; Musaf, the additional service; and Concluding. Maishe was quite familiar with these obligations and prayed in both Hebrew and English.

Selected Bibliography:

Barton, Clara. The Story of my Childhood. New York: Arno Press Inc., 1980.

Diethrich, Edward B., M.D. "The Sternal Saw: A Historical Note with a Modern Message." Letter. *The Journal of Thoracic and Cardiovascular Surgery*. V. 107, no. 4, p. 1157f, 2011.

Head, Stuart J. et. Al. "Coronary Artery Bypass Grafting . . . The Evolution Over the First 50 Years." *European Heart Journal*. Vol. 34, Is 37, pp. 2862-2872, 1 October 2013.

Letterman, Jonathan. *Medical Recollections of the Army of the Potomac*. New York: D Appleton [at Google Books], 1866.

Musto, R. J. "The Treatment of the Wounded at Gettysburg: Jonathan Letterman: The Father of Modern Battlefield Medicine." *Gettysburg Magazine*. Is. 37, 2007.

Phillips, Natalie and Ana Gattet. "Open Heart Surgery." *Healthline.com*. Retrieved June, 2018.

Pryor, Elizabeth Brown. *Clara Barton, Professional Angel*. Philadelphia: University of Pennsylvania Press, 1988.

Ruelas, Richard. "Ted Diethrich, Famed Heart Surgeon, Dead at 81." Obit. *The Republic*. March 2, 2017. Online.

www.ingramcontent.com/pod-product-compliance
Lightning Source LLC
Chambersburg PA
CBHW021429070526
44577CB00001B/124